FINANCIAL

Longevity

FINANCIAL

Longevity

**Your
Guide to
Securing
Your
Family's
Financial
Future**

DAN OWENS

Financial Longevity: Your Guide to Securing Your Family's
Financial Future
Copyright © 2019 by Danterious Owens
All rights reserved

Printed in the United States of America

First Printing, 2019

ISBN: 9781798862667

Danterious Owens
Dallas, TX
Email: DanTheMentor@yahoo.com
www.DanTheMentor.com

Editor: Jason Whited, www.Jason-Whited.com

Book cover designer: Lew Donley, Tentact,
www.tentactonline.com

Editor/proofreader and interior book designer: Jean Boles
https://www.upwork.com/fl/jeanboles

Dedication

This book is dedicated to my grandfather and grandmother, Roosevelt and Ada, my paternal grandmother, Joyce, and my mother, Erica, my fiancé, Glorieuse, and my son, Danterious Jr.

"Live like no one else, so later you can live and give like no one else."

– Dave Ramsey

Contents

Preface

First and foremost, I want to thank you and extend my tremendous appreciation to you for purchasing *Financial Longevity*! In this book, you will develop a strong financial foundation to catapult you and your family's personal finances to the next level. I have divulged every ounce of knowledge that has been gifted to me by mentors, academic scholars, books, financial experts, and from the prestigious school of hard knocks.

I remember being overwhelmed—in thousands of dollars' worth of debt, having a below average credit rating, and trying to raise a toddler as a single parent after fighting an expensive custody battle. During those same times of tribulation, I remember working over 80 hours a week, graduating from college with a 3.2 GPA, doing my *Debt Free Scream* on the *Dave Ramsey Show,* and starting my business, Dan The Mentor. I understand how hard it can be during struggles and difficult times, and I wanted to create this book as a guide, containing easy to understand strategies and hope for everyday hard- working people.

Upon conclusion of this book, you will have an in-depth understanding of personal finance, credit, investing, estate planning, and many more financial topics that we will uncover in the coming chapters. My life's mission is to help as many people as I possibly can to charter their Financial Longevity journey!

Again, I want to send a big thank you for purchasing this book; I believe you will enjoy reading it and applying the knowledge and tips inside toward your own financial success! Let's get focused!

Chapter 1: Start

When embarking on any financial journey, we sometimes tend to think of the process as a complex algorithm or something akin to a calculus class. However, the number one reason why most people fail at becoming financially free is...brace yourself: a failure to start.

Now you can breathe. Not what you expected? Think of the last time you decided to begin a healthy diet or pursue another career. How long did it take you to officially start, or did the process of starting even materialize? This is important to keep in mind because you have successfully passed the first obstacle, which is starting—and you fulfilled this by purchasing this book and actually turning to the first page. Congratulations!

Your first step is to get together with your spouse/partner, or if you're single, to grab an accountability partner, if needed. This is important. If you're in a committed relationship, it means both of you are on the same team and trying to win. If the two of you are not on the same page, it's going to be like the Patriots versus Rams in the Super Bowl: a tough, competitive game against each other while both are trying to win and reach their own goal. So, both of you have to start with the same mindset, team vision, and goals.

I'm old fashioned for my age, but I prefer to have a nice pen and paper when it comes to organizing or planning things. I typically input the data in an app/computer later on—but do what works best for you.

Then, you will sit down with your partner to discuss what your dreams are, what kind of legacy you want to leave, where you want to be in your career five, ten, and maybe twenty years from now. Most importantly, you want to think about what your life would look like if money wasn't an issue. Answering that question will reveal your true passions and goals. This is a valuable step that you can use to hold yourself accountable in the event of disagreements or arguments. You can refer to these same goals and say, "Hey, whose opinion most aligns with our long-term goals?" Does the other person's argument delay our goals or accelerate them? Not only will this debunk arguments, but it will keep you motivated throughout this journey.

I bet you thought this process was going to be easy. Not quite! You can expect a lot of conversations with your spouse or close friends about this change in lifestyle. Remember, approximately 50 percent of Americans are living paycheck to paycheck, according to a report by CNBC. Furthermore, almost 69 percent have an emergency fund that's less than $1,000, according to Forbes.com. And, believe me, nobody is going into debt to invest in some sort of new startup that is going to be the next Apple or Amazon company. A lot of this debt is bad debt. You can learn a lot of about bad debt by reading Robert Kiyosaki's book *Rich Dad Poor Dad.*

After drafting your goals and long-term plan(s) for the future, it's time to create a written budget that allocates your monthly income to your monthly expenses. This budget promotes a good habit in that it encourages you to think of your money each month without overspending on unnecessary items/services. So, begin by writing down your current bills, expenses, and other financial obligations. If you feel technologically savvy and adept, you can download apps like Mint, EveryDollar (which financial expert Dave Ramsey highly recommends) or create a straightforward Excel document. Also, if applicable, combine you and your spouse's net monthly income. After inputting all the recurring monthly expense, subtract the total expenses from your income to discover if you're overspending. If so, adjust and cut out items you don't need.

The budget is an essential part of the process. Think of a budget as if you are running a business. Sales minus expenses equal profit. If your expenses (output), are more than your income/sales (input), you will have a negative profit. If this continues, it will cause your business to fail and, in some cases, go bankrupt.

This scenario is applied to personal finance the same exact way. If you don't create a budget and continue to overspend without repositioning your expenditures, your personal life will fail and possibly go bankrupt, causing stress and hardship within the family, workplace, and sometimes bad health and suicide.

Even I had to Start Somewhere

I hope to bring tremendous value to you and your family's life by passing on this book and assisting you as much as I can with all the information I have learned over the years. By no means do I consider myself a financial guru or some sort of know it all. I simply want to help empower people to take control of their financial life. The best way I can do this is by giving my testimony and how I managed to achieve a debt-free, minimalistic lifestyle.

I remember looking at my financial statement for the first time, and after deducting all my obligations, I was negative $65,000 in total net worth. I struggled to grasp the situation and sought financial help. Everywhere I searched, I saw get-rich-quick schemes or some financial guru trying to sell me a bad product. In some instances, people were trying to get me to invest money in their product by maxing out my credit cards and promising me some great returns on my money. So, I realized I had to formulate my own plan.

I started making short YouTube videos, mini blogs, and even social media posts to get the information out, but no one seemed to be interested. It's as if everyone was in some sort of financial matrix controlled by an outside source. I read books, watched documentaries, and even travelled to different places to see what was so complicated about one being financially free. I researched to see what the millionaires, billionaires, and other financial experts are doing that is so different from everyone else that causes them to be wealthy. While searching for answers, it seemed as though everyone else was caught up in extreme consumerism, avoiding delayed gratification and worried about celebrities and some professional sports game the previous night.

But wait, this isn't about me and my weird life observations. I am supposed to be assisting you with financial literacy and getting you into the financially free lifestyle. So, let's get to it.

Credit Report

After completing your budget, the next thing I want you to do is to check your credit report from all three credit bureaus. Even if you do not possess any debt, obtaining a credit report is critical, especially in this time of hacking and cyberattacks. As I write this paragraph of the book, we recently experienced an Equifax data breach that affected half of the American population, roughly one hundred and forty-three million people! And to my unpleasant surprise, I was affected! And there is probably a 50 percent-plus chance you were affected as well, so get on it ASAP. Even consider putting a freeze on all of your credit reports and temporarily unfreeze when applying for lines on credit that require an inquiry from that specific bureau. This may cost a few dollars, but it is well worth it to prevent fraud.

The three credit bureaus are Equifax, Transunion, and Experian. Again, this could change in the future, so be sure to stay up to date on the latest news on any upcoming credit bureaus. It is always your responsibility to keep track of this information because in the event there is an error, or if someone misused your information, you could be held accountable if the problem is not taken care of swiftly. The burden of proof usually lies with the consumer in some of these situations where you delay reporting fraudulent activity or credit report errors.

I have worked with a number of people who opened up lines of credit in their child's name and I have had to help them repair their credit. Sad story.

I am in no way affiliated or work for Credit Karma; however, I personally use their services to obtain my Transunion and Equifax credit reports and scores for FREE. They give monthly updates on any changes to both reports and provide insight to what is lowering your credit score. You can also file your taxes with Credit Karma, compare credit cards, and see which lines of credit you have a good chance on getting approved for. The entire site sort of knocks out two birds with one stone essentially. (https://www.creditkarma.com/)

After completing this step, even though you have checked all three reports, continue to make it a habit to check at least once a month. Most people say check it every six months or once a year, but here's my inner finance nerd showing again: I believe in preventative maintenance, so if you check every month, you can catch any problems or errors ahead of time versus catching them later and wrestling with the credit agencies and the financial institution that created the mess. Trust me, it's worth taking five minutes once a month to make sure everything checks out.

Once you've assessed of all your credit reports, reevaluate your budget to make sure you included all of your debt obligations and include any stragglers, if needed. We haven't made it to this step in the process yet, but be sure to only list your minimum payments in the debt payments category of your budget. When your budget is completed, you should be able to identify two items:

1. Where a majority of your income is being allocated
2. A total amount of cash left.

Statistically, in most cases, the total amount of cash left is in the negative, but that's OK. Remember, over 60 percent of Americans live paycheck to paycheck, so you are not alone. Don't feel embarrassed; we have all been there. Even me.

Revising the Budget

Did I mention there is a second budget? This will be the new and improved budget. First, take a look at your original budget that you previously drafted. Most are shocked to see that they were spending more on a car note than their own rent or mortgage. In some instances, the car insurance is more than the freaking car payment, and you may very well find yourself in this predicament. This is all normal and OK, so breathe.

Inhale...Exhale...Inhale...Exhale.

All right, time to roll up your sleeves and get to the hard work. Fair warning: Your partner or spouse may not sleep well after tonight. We are going to perform surgery on all your expense, essentially cutting out all the bad items, reducing the good ones, and maintaining the ones out of our control. Now that doesn't mean to leave the cable and unlimited data plan because you "need" entertainment and Facebook. Bye-bye, internet, cable, restaurants, movies, new clothes, new phones, etc. Oh, and by the way, if that car has payments on it, we are getting rid of it and downsizing to a beater. But wait, there's more. No more malls, expensive family vacations, bachelor parties, Black Friday shopping, and store-closure sales.

After reading those short three sentences, I bet half you closed the book or are continuing to read for the *Oh, I was just joking* moment. Nope, sorry, I am not joking. In fact, I am so serious and I am here to tell you that your life depends on you creating this budget and sticking to it.

Obviously, everyone's personal situation differs. However, it is crucial that you take this step seriously and cut back on everything you don't need temporarily until you obtain financial freedom and can afford these First World luxuries.

OK, I'm done; you can continue reading again.

After cutting out all expenses, you should see a big difference in your new budget. If not, you may not have cut deeply enough. If you have any leftover cash, we will get to how to put that to use later on in this book.

Here is an example of how your budget should look. Feel free use this page as draft for your budget:

BUDGET

Type of Payment	Amount
Rent/Mortgage:	$
Utilities (Water, Gas, Electric, etc.):	$
Phone:	$
Groceries:	$
Credit Card 1 Payment:	$
Credit Card 2 Payment:	$
Auto Loan:	$
Other Debt Payments (Minimum Payment Due):	$
Transportation (Gas, Insurance, Parking, Maintenance):	$
Daycare:	$
Alimony/Child Support:	$
Retirement [401(k), IRA, 403(b), etc.]:	$
Health/Life Insurance:	$
Internet:	$
Pet Expenses:	$
Miscellaneous:	$
Total Income:	$
(Minus) Total Expenses:	$
(Equals) Total Cash left over:	$
(Direct total cash left over to debt or savings. More info in Chapter 2)	
Total Assets/Everything you own outright that has value:	$
(Minus) Total Debt/Liabilities/ Financial Obligations:	$
(Equals) Net worth:	$

The list of items within your budget can be longer or shorter depending on how many expenses you have. List every obligation you have to meet each month.

To simplify your total amount of assets, just add big-ticket items such as your bank account balances, cars you own, retirement funds, home, etc. Don't include couches, TVs, beds, etc.

Negotiate for Lower Rates

Just a few quick tips before finishing your budget: It is always OK to call your insurance agent and ask for a "re-rate" on your policy for a lower premium, which may cause it to decrease or increase, depending on your record—and nowadays, even your credit score. You can shop around with other insurance companies using an insurance broker to give you the most competitive pricing. Be mindful, though, that sometimes cheapest isn't best. Make sure your coverage is enough to protect you in case of a lawsuit and can cover the replacement of your vehicle and possibly the other vehicles that may be involved in an accident. Only deal with reputable companies with excellent track records that pay their claims quickly and accurately.

I can't tell you the numerous situations I encounter where someone is paying for full coverage insurance on a vehicle that is over ten years old. Everyone, please do not exceed the amount of coverage you actually need on your car that is only worth a few thousand dollars. If your car is worth $2,000, for instance, you only need liability coverage and you can go buy another car with your emergency savings.

Speaking of cars—don't you dare go visit another dealership unless you are the one selling your vehicle. I'm sorry to hurt your feelings, but cars depreciate and are probably the worst financial purchase people make of all time. (Deprecation occurs when something reduces in market value. Appreciation occurs when something increases in market value). I don't care if it has a one-million-mile warranty. The moment you drive the car off the lot, it reduces more than 20% in value and you are stuck paying interest to the bank you borrowed money from to buy the car. A car is a tool that transports you from one destination to the next. There is no reason to allow a car to suck up half of your income for the sake of looking good.

My recommendation: Buy a used car that is in good condition with cash. During this phase when you are trying to get out debt, steer clear of dealerships. If your car is taking up a large part of your budget, sell it and transition to a cheaper car. Trust me, I hated getting rid of all of my nice toys, but we are adults and only children need toys to play with.

Another area to cut back that some people forget is internet, cable, phone, and other services. Sometimes when calling the cable/internet company, you can threaten to cancel, and they will reduce your bill or offer free services for a certain time period. What do you have to lose from calling?

You can additionally download some saving apps like Walmart's Savings Catcher or join Target's Red Card program, and you will get discounts and cash back to use later in the store. There are many ways to reduce your current expenses, often just by picking up the phone or receiving certain memberships, but don't fall for store offers to open a new credit card. Those will only cause you to spend more money within the store on products you don't need.

This is all to say, most of your recurring expenses are up for negotiation, even the electric bill. Try giving all the companies you listed within your budget a call to negotiate a lower bill. Switching to a different company in some cases can lead to increased savings, since most institutions are competing for market share. I remember switching phone companies simply because one was willing to buy me out of the other and offered me a cheaper bill. This saved me hundreds of dollars down the road.

Even though it may seem as if you are negotiating for dollars and cents, last time I checked, dollars could add up to hundreds of dollars, and hundreds of dollars could add up to thousands of dollars. The first step to becoming wealthy is understanding that every dollar is important, no matter how small the amount is. A dollar today increases in value over time when invested instead of consumed.

Tax Withholdings

Another overlooked area of most people's budget is their tax withholdings from their paycheck. If you are employed by a company, you filled out a tax form called a W-4. Within this form you elected allowances and other "extra" deductions you want taken out of your check. If this form is completed correctly, you should receive little to no tax refund at the end of the year. Yes, the goal is to have Uncle

Sam refund you as little money as possible or none at all. When you receive a refund, this usually means you overpaid in taxes and the government owes you that amount back. The inconvenient part is this: The IRS does not have to pay any interest on the money they have held from you all year. They also don't have to work to give you the maximum amount they owe you. It is your job as a taxpayer to become familiar with tax law or hire a CPA (Certified Public Accountant) to make sure you are paying the correct amount in taxes each year.

It's very important to go back and check your W-4 to make sure you are withholding the appropriate amount of allowances. Once corrected, you should be able to see an increase in your paychecks. This money can be used to save, invest, or pay off your debt. Be sure to talk to your accountant for more information.

A final note regarding your budget. If you find yourself truly exceeding your budget after decreasing all expenses and your housing takes up more than 30 percent of your income, I have one word: relocate.

To give you a bigger picture, the most expensive items of most Americans' budget are housing, transportation, and food. If you have kids, that would come in as the second largest expense. These should be major areas of focus when revising the budget.

You don't have to continuously pay high rent to remain in the area you are in. Just move to a cheaper location and try to reduce your housing costs that way. If you are locked in to a mortgage, maybe listing your home for sale is the next step. Getting a roommate, downsizing, or renting out the spare bedroom are also good cost-saving strategies! Regardless of your housing situation, never feel as though you are stuck. You are never locked down to one location.

Maybe you have children; instead of paying costly school tuition fees to a private school, enroll your child in public school. I've even started to see people homeschool their children more often or have one parent stay at home to cut back on daycare costs.

Remember, these are the greatest impacted areas of your budget, so do not be afraid to dial back these expenses temporarily for the greater goal!

This budget is not final and will not be the budget you use permanently throughout this process. We are simply organizing your finances to optimize your income for the coming steps. Once you have the budget instilled in your mind, you will eventually be able to adhere to it by habit, without drafting a new one each month. I hope that this gives you a clear picture on where your money has been going and ways to best put it to use.

Boring Old Insurance Can Create Exciting Benefits

Now that your new and improved budget is complete and you have successfully reduced and cut out unnecessary expenses, it's time for you to set up life, health, long-term disability, and other insurance coverage that may be applicable in your personal circumstances.

Beginning with life insurance, you will have several options, such as 'whole life' insurance, or what is called 'term coverage.' Most financial experts recommend term life Insurance due to its low cost and simplification. You simply select a reputable company, a term length that is applicable with your personal goals/situation, and an insurable amount that you are comfortable leaving behind for your beneficiaries. If you are young, this would be an ideal time to purchase because you will have absolutely the lowest premium possible rather than waiting until you are sixty, when coverage may not even be an option or available. And to all my wise elders who are reading, it's never too late to set up a life insurance policy even though the premium may be higher. However, due to your tremendous wisdom, I am sure you have accumulated assets such as a home, an IRA/401(k), a pension, etc. You have the option to select beneficiaries for these accounts, and this can act as a life insurance policy, as well, in the event of your death.

Which brings me to part two of setting up life insurance. You will have to set up a meeting with a professional estate attorney to create a will, powers of attorney, a trust, etc. These are important because in the event you are incapacitated or no longer alive, your love ones and family members will need specific direction instructing them on how to distribute your assets. This also important because you will decide how you want your medical care to be handled, and your burial preference. Very important.

Depending on the current tax laws, you may have to visit with an accountant and seek advice on how to structure your estate and to distribute assets. There could be a significant amount of taxes due if not structured and distributed correctly. Some may find that leaving 100 percent to a spouse is more beneficial for tax purposes; others may find it easier to gift their assets away while they are still alive. So, please seek professional advice on this step so that you achieve the best results.

Another important piece of wisdom from this step is that this alleviates the possibility of a broken family and drama. When you leave everything disorganized and without instruction, this leaves space for arguments and a nasty fight, damaging or destroying the family tree for generations. In my personal life, I remember both of my grandfathers' deaths. The only thing on everyone's mind was who gets the Corvette? Who gets the Camaro? Who gets the assets? Who gets the savings account? Just chaos. Families should be bonding and healing, not fighting over material goods.

What did both my grandfathers have in common upon their death? They did not establish an estate and a will with instructions, consequently leaving a bitter legacy behind and broken family trees. So, please spend time and go over this with an estate attorney, establish instructions, and if needed, have a family meeting if you become ill and discuss the intricacies of the estate you established.

Moving on to health insurance, you can either apply for coverage through your employer's plan, a third party, or the government if you are in poverty status or eligible for government-offered programs. There isn't much information to cover here, but make sure that you do have coverage in case you are hospitalized. Too many times have I witnessed clients who lacked health coverage face extremely high medical bills that eventually went to collections. This can cause additional stress on top of being hospitalized.

Furthermore, you can purchase long-term disability insurance, which will come in handy at times where you are unable to produce income. It's easy to neglect the thought of becoming disabled while you are in excellent health, but there is always uncertainty. Moreover, adding another insurance product, such as long-term care is also not bad option.

Remember, the insurance section is completely optional, but I want you to at least take a look at it, research, and find out if your situation calls for it.

If you are a young adult between ages eighteen to thirty-five, now is the best time to lock in life insurance since premiums are extremely cheap at this age, probably cheaper than a pair of jeans. If you wait until you're fifty or sixty, it will be significantly more expensive.

Out of all these products, I encourage young adults to at least purchase life insurance. If you are over the age of thirty-five, purchase life insurance even though it is more expensive.

Overall, it is always a good time to explore the additional insurance products I mentioned above. The main idea is to assess your life, observe the risks, implement a plan, and have insurance just in case plans don't quite work out the way you had in mind.

Congratulations, this brings us to the start of your very first steps toward financial longevity. Loads of information covered, but remember that starting is the toughest part for the "ordinary." Let's be extraordinary. This would probably be a great time to pause and implement the first step. I wanted to write this book in a certain order to allow you to follow along as you go through each process. So, feel free to proceed to the next chapter or take time to cover what I've already outlined. Let's Go! Time to make an impact and change your family legacy!

Chapter 2: Rainy Day/Inconvenience Fund

Earlier, I mentioned that approximately 60 percent of Americans live paycheck to paycheck and lack at least $1,000 cash for an emergency. This is absolutely not safe and can be quite dangerous under the right conditions and variables. In this chapter, we will discuss setting up a partial emergency savings account or—as I would like to call it—a Rainy Day/Inconvenience Fund.

I remember as a child growing up in the '90s to early 2000s, cash and checks were pretty common; however, credit was becoming the main source of spending and making transactions. This is when the internet was ramping up and online shopping was available but not as widespread as it is now. We didn't have the "one-click-to-buy" option that we see on Amazon, Walmart, and other online retail leaders. There was no such thing as free two-day shipping and same-day delivery. As we saw the use of credit and debit cards rise, I saw less and less cash in circulation. All you see today is 0 percent financing, instant store credit approval, no credit checks, and the list goes on. This is all a mind game that psychologists researched and studied for decades. Retailers paid psychologists for their research to figure out a way to make more sales to impulsive consumers. Maybe the famous public intellectual Noam Chomsky said it best:

"Take a course in economics, they tell you a market is based on informed consumers making rational choices. Anyone who's ever looked at a TV ad knows that's not true…The goal is to undermine markets by creating uninformed consumers who will make irrational choices…"

I want my readers to go back to the Stone Age and hold some cash for a rainy day, just like grandma used to tell us to do. Crazy, right? Well, way back in 1940 Grandma was speaking wisdom for the twenty-first century.

Savings Accounts

First, I want you to shop around for a high-yield savings account. You can find basic savings accounts at the big banks like Bank of America, Chase, and Citi. However, also check with your local credit unions, online banks, or smaller local banks. Online banks usually offer significantly higher interest on your savings than the big banks and brick-and-mortar institutions. I have found that my highest APY (Annual Percentage Yield) was at my employer's credit union and with a major online bank. The reason online banks are able to offer a higher APY on their savings accounts is because they don't operate out of expensive physical locations that require as many employees, equipment, maintenance, and other expenses. They make banking easy for everyone by offering access to thousands of ATMs, and some offer reimbursement for any fees incurred from withdrawing cash. Customer service is usually 24/7. Perhaps best of all, you can easily access your account from your phone to transfer or send money, deposit checks, or apply for other products they offer. No more driving to the bank wasting gas and precious daylight!

Take note, though: Do not deposit this cash in a CD (Certificate of Deposit) or brokerage account. The point of an emergency fund is to be able to withdraw money quickly for emergency use. So, when setting up your account at the institution of your choosing, make sure to only open an interest-earning savings account that will allow you 24/7 access to your cash. Preferably, choose an institution that you currently don't have a checking account with. We want to make sure that this money is out of sight, out of mind.

Furthermore, if you opt to use your local bank, you are supporting your community and won't be treated like a number or statistic in their system. I notice many financial experts just say open a savings account anywhere, but I like to be thorough. Instead of telling you to just make uninformed choices on where you do business, I want you to actually do the research and support places that want to support you.

Investing your savings with these types of institutions pays off down the road because, first and foremost, you are supporting them. Second, you are establishing history. Finally, you just never know when you may need a personal, business, or mortgage loan from them. They may be your most cost-effective option if you ever decide to go any of those routes later in life. Some are willing to work with you simply because of your history of business and your continued support, not solely rejecting you on a credit score.

I would further say that it's important to do research on the businesses you decide to bank with because of past scandals such as what happened at Wells Fargo. It's interesting that I called them years ago about an account that was opened with my social security number and the representative would say the account existed. However, once I was forwarded to the fraud department, they would say no such account existed with my social security number. About a year later, news broke that Wells Fargo had people in the inside that were creating fake accounts. I was a victim, and they are offering a settlement to those that were affected. So, do the research before doing business with anyone you'd like to trust to hold your hard-earned money.

Rainy Days Do Happen

After deciding upon a bank/credit union to open your initial savings account, our goal is to save at least one month's pay or one month's worth of expenses. This can range anywhere between $500-$5,000 or more if you are making over six figures in income. If your income fluctuates or for some reason you did not organize a budget in Chapter 1, Dave Ramsey recommends starting with $1,000, which is a great amount to start with. I always recommend one month's savings because there isn't always a one-size-fits-all approach when it comes to finances. Remember, this is not a fully funded emergency fund; this is just a partial amount to have saved in case of minor emergencies that may happen as you work through the next steps in this process.

Some may wonder what's the point in creating a partial emergency fund instead of just knocking it out and creating a fully funded one. If you have a majority mindset, you may even say, "Why do I need an emergency fund when I have my credit cards for emergencies?"

These are all valid questions, and I respect those perspectives. However, to answer the first question, we have to have a partial emergency fund to prevent stepping back during the debt-free process. If you are fully energized, and start making progress on your debt, the car may break down and now you need $1,000 in repairs. This will instantly kill your motivation.

Maybe your hours on the job are cut for a week and you need $500 to cover the utility bills; now you have to swipe that credit card that you almost paid off to cover your expenses. Again, destroying your stride.

There are so many unknown variables that could happen, and usually these situations cause pause, stress, and feelings of defeat. If you have that partial emergency savings as backup, you won't be stressed and can continue the process without any interruptions setting you back.

To answer the second question regarding using credit cards for emergencies, this is a horrible idea to begin with. If you are already in debt or in a tough situation, don't add more fuel to flame by further trapping yourself. Some people get the feeling of temporary relief when they use credit cards, debt-consolidation loans, HELOCs (Home Equity Lines of Credit), etc. But the key word is *temporary*. Once you fall back down to reality, you will then encounter the same problem and stress times two. I'm not trying to beat up those who believe this is a solution, but I cannot stress enough how dangerous that plan can become. Let's face the problem and tackle it head-on and get rid of it. Forever!

Depending on your personal situation, you may barely be bringing in enough income to cover your living expenses. This could make the process of funding your partial emergency saving account a tad bit tougher. No worries, I will try to share a few solutions to this problem below.

Bump Up that Income
First, are you making the absolute maximum amount of income possible in relation to your skill set, educational competitiveness, tenure, current job market, etc.? You could be an awesome web designer, but you work in a call center (nothing is wrong with working in a call center, awesome job!). But you could start creating websites on the side for businesses and increase your streams of income.

Let's take another example: Maybe you have a master's degree in psychology, but you work as a social worker. Well, you could open your own practice on the side or possibly teach college-level courses as an adjunct professor.

Sometimes people stay loyal to one job and accumulate years of seniority and become a valuable asset to the company they work for when they *could* negotiate a salary increase or apply for other internal opportunities. What I'm trying to say is, don't box yourself, or your career, in.

You can even shop around for external job opportunities and choose a company that aligns more with your personal and long-term goals.

There was an article posted on Forbes in 2014 that stated, "Employees who stay in companies longer than two years get paid 50 percent less." Wow, talk about boxing yourself in, right? With the economic unpredictability of recent decades, retiring at a company after forty years doesn't seem to be the most economical route anymore. And while that's not the case 100 percent of the time, it won't hurt to consider other options outside of your current place of employment.

The most impactful way to move the needle when it comes to building up your emergency fund, getting out debt, and investing is your income. I'm not saying panic and resign from your job tomorrow, but have a projected outlook on how much your income will grow in the future. Inflation grows at an average rate of three to five percent each year, which means your income has to grow at a rate as fast or faster than inflation in order to prevent a decrease in your annual buying power (Inflation is the annual cost increase of goods and services). That's why it's important to not become complacent during your career.

For those who may be 100 percent happy with their current job and do not want to change anything about it, there are always other strategies.

You can host a garage sale. If you have an abundance of stuff around the house that you no longer need, you could have a garage sale every weekend until you exhaust all the excess you possess. This can strengthen your emergency savings and may lead to a large lump sum of cash.

Perhaps you or your spouse is a stay-at-home parent; you can start babysitting other working parents' children along with your own. I have seen people charge anywhere from $10 an hour to $30-plus an hour for just taking care of the kiddos on the weekend while the parents catch a break. Some people may even accommodate you with a place to stay within their home to be a 24/7 nanny/babysitter. That means no rent, grocery bill, and you are getting paid a decent wage. Not a bad option if you are single person. Could get a little weird if you are married and attempt to stay at someone's home as a full-time nanny, though. Again, not every possible solution will apply to you.

Another option to quickly achieve the one month's savings is to shop around for cash-back checking/savings accounts. I have signed up for one in the past that offered me $300 just for signing up for direct deposit in the first ninety days. You can do this with two banks, and there you could have $600 in a matter of weeks!

There are also surveys that pay you a few cents or dollars just for a few minutes of your time. Do a hundred a day, and you may just have a few hundred dollars in a couple months. I have used Inbox Dollars, Google Ads, and sometimes I will upload personal reviews on products I have used and put a link to the item using an Amazon link to get commission for all of my referrals.

You can cut yards during the summer, rake leaves in the fall, shovel snow in the winter, and plant flowers in the spring for neighbors and the local citizens in your community for a low overhead cost. I did this when I was sixteen and made lots of money—plus tips—since I charged such a low price for my labor.

Finally, if you are set to receive a tax refund at the beginning of the year, save that toward your Rainy-Day Fund.

Bottom Line

The bottom line is that there are an immeasurable number of things to do to make some extra income, whether it is in the community, online, or just by using your flexible schedule to help others by providing value to their personal life.

This step may take a few weeks to a few months to complete, so don't become discouraged if you don't make fistfuls of money instantly. Also, continue to invest in your retirement accounts up to your employer match if possible. This is essentially free money left on the table. If your employer matches up to $1,000, then only put $1,000 in for that year to get the match. Once you have met the match, discontinue investing in retirement and allocate the rest of that cash to your Rainy Day Fund. I made the mistake of not continuously investing up to my employer match and missed out on the free money I would have received—

thousands of dollars left on the table. Don't make the mistake I did.

Furthermore, if your employer provides time-off benefits, start saving in this step toward the maximum, or correlate the amount of time off with what I call your Stormy Day Fund, which is your fully funded emergency savings. (Chapter 4)

When I was hired with one of my employers, my goal was to take as little time off as I could to create a buffer on top of my emergency savings. There, employees accrued time based on the number of hours worked. If you worked twenty hours/pay-period, this would translate into three hours of paid time off (PTO) in your time-off bank. Forty hours hours/pay-period translated into six and a half hours in your PTO bank. The maximum accrual amount was approximately 320 hours for new employees with one to five years' seniority, which was a total of forty days off (two months). I saved the maximum of forty days, which will allow me to continue to receive paychecks every two weeks post-employment until I completely exhausted my PTO bank. When I decide to switch employers, I will essentially receive a bonus on top of my new employer's paycheck. In case of emergencies that may cause me to separate from my employer, I will have a total of two months' emergency savings.

Don't rely on this for emergencies instead of saving for your Rainy Day/Stormy Day Fund; this is just a strategy to use to create an extra buffer and margin of error for the worst-case scenarios. This is optional, but I highly recommend starting to save the extra PTO on top of your savings. Too many times have I witnessed coworkers struggle to stay at home with a sick child, or visit a loved one that is ill, because they lacked PTO and couldn't afford taking the day off without pay. It will be hard to not take those two-week vacations right when your bank is reloaded, but remember Chapter 1, when you created your long-term goals. The best part of this strategy is that once you save the initial amount of PTO, you have to take days off because you either saved the maximum or have enough for emergencies that take long periods of time.

Be sure to check with your employer's human resources department on their PTO policy to ensure that you are entitled to receive a payment equivalent to the amount PTO you accrued in the event you separate from the company. Moreover, ask if there are restrictions to the amount of PTO you can accrue and if you will lose it if you don't use it in a timely manner. Always read the company policies and benefits to make sure you are following their guidelines and taking advantage of all other potential benefits.

Life is a Marathon
Life is a marathon, just hold steady and be consistent. Remember to talk to your accountability partner, whether it's your spouse, close friend, or parent. They are there to keep you on track and to assist in times of discouragement. Sometimes if you keep a positive social circle of people that are familiar with your financial freedom journey, they may help you connect with people who are employers or someone looking for a service that you may offer. It's

almost like networking, getting connected with people who can make the process smoother and give you those healthy bumps up.

You never know if the person next to you is an owner of a business, leader of a church, accountant, realtor, or just another person traveling a similar path as you in life. I have surely met great people throughout my life that gave me those small assists that meant the world to me. One of my mentors offered me $200 one day just to help me in a situation and time of need that I was in. I would have never expected it, but I am thankful every day that person was there at that specific time of my life. So, you all may be wondering why I'm rambling about this; but I only want to point out the importance of just being a good person no matter what obstacles you are facing. You can start with a simple smile, a good morning, etc. You never know who that one person will be to change your life. Sermon concluded!

Now, once you have completed your partial savings account, you can move forward to paying off your debt. It can seem easy to throw this money you have saved at debt or to spend it on some expensive gadgets or clothes, but pretend that the money isn't there. If possible, don't link this account to your primary checking account. Keep this account by itself with its own bank or credit union, and let it sit there until an emergency arises.

I know it has been tough, and these first few steps are probably major changes to your life, but keep the discipline and stay the course. When I reached this point, it was the most money I had seen in my bank account in my life. Every day it was tempting to use this cash to buy a new gadget or go back to swiping my credit card. As a matter of fact, I did just that. I bought a new phone shortly after reaching this point but promised I myself I would get serious. I know it's sad, but I never said I was perfect.

You ever ask your parent why did they do something they always told you not to? And they always responded, "Do as I say, not as I do" or "I'm the grownup and you're the child." This is that situation right here. Just follow my recommendation, and only use this cash for legitimate emergencies.

We all stumble and fall short of doing exactly as we'd planned, but the important part is getting back up to continue the process. Though this process can become rigorous, remember to refer back to your *why* and the reason you are doing all of this. That will be your source for strength to pull through.

Chapter 3: Tackle All Debt/Financial Obligations: Student Loans, Credit Cards, and Collections

In this next chapter, we will be discussing the next level in your financially free journey: eliminating all debt and financial obligations except the mortgage. This will include any and everything you owe, from auto loans, student loans, and credit cards to collections, judgments, delinquent accounts, etc. I have watched on TV and read insane articles advising people not to pay certain bills, or how to "get away" without paying old accounts, medical bills, etc. Trust me, you know what I am talking about. From an honest and moral perspective, I believe in paying what you owe; therefore, I advise my readers to always pay what you owe. Yes, there may be loopholes in a contract or agreement that allow you to not pay certain bills. Yes, there are times when collections and judgments don't appear on your credit report. But that doesn't clear the aspect that overall this is called stealing. No matter how you "cleared" or "bypassed" the system, you still owe that person or business the amount you are responsible for.

Wouldn't it upset you if a catastrophe happened to your car, and the insurance company refused to pay what they owe you because of some loophole in the forms you signed? I am pretty sure 99 percent of you would be furious. So, pay what you owe forward and move on. Who wants these debts hanging over their head for years and constantly going to court for $500? I have seen people avoid paying $500—not to say that that isn't a lot of money—but come on, people, is that $500 headache really worth it? List EVERYTHING. Even what you owe Cousin Leroy around the corner.

By now, you should have a good idea of all the debts and financial obligations you owe if you completed Step 1. You also should have obtained all your credit reports and implemented your debt payments into your budget.

If you have a workbook or an app you are using, go ahead and open that now. I want you to write down all your debts from the smallest balance to the largest. If you are married, this will include your spouse's debts as well. Include the interest rate, minimum payment, and the length of the loan if applicable. Typically, collections do not have an interest or minimum payment, they will just have a balance and a lot of fees added in, but I will teach you how to handle that later on in this chapter, so hold tight. Do not include your mortgage in this step of the process.

Debt Payoff Strategies

Once you have all of your debts listed, there are three methods I suggest on how to pay them off. The first method is the *Psychological Method*, which is taught by Dave

Ramsey. You will pay the minimum payment due on all the debts. Then whatever is extra left out of your monthly budget will go to the smallest balance completely. This is also called the *Debt Snowball*. As you pay down the smallest debts, you will get instant gratification and continue on until you finally knock out the largest. The reason it is called a Debt Snowball is because after you are done paying off the smallest debt, you have that minimum payment now added to your cash flow, which is the money you have left each month in your budget. The snowball gets bigger and bigger as you pay off the small ones, causing you to have a lot more cash to throw at the largest debt, consequently knocking it out quicker than starting with the largest first. If you haven't caught on yet, Dave Ramsey is one of my mentors that I have tremendous respect for, so I will be referencing him quite often in this book along with others. I have to give all of them credit for their genius pieces of work and ideas.

The key to making the Debt Snowball work is to get fired up and tackle the debts like a football player in the final seconds of the fourth quarter. Stay intense, and before you know it you will be debt free. If you find yourself discouraged or burned out, just look at your long-term goals and talk to your motivation partner or coach to crank the inspiration back up. It's important to remember the reason for all of this. Whether it is building generational wealth, early retirement, or just keeping your family secure and safe in hard times. The why is as important as the execution through the process.

A Debt Snowball list of debts should look similar to this:
Debt 1: $100 (Minimum Payment = $30/Month)
Debt 2: $1,000 (Minimum Payment = $75/Month)
Debt 3: $5,000 (Minimum Payment = $200/Month)
Debt 4: $8,000 (Minimum Payment = $350/Month), and so forth…

Leftover cash from your budget in Chapter 1 goes toward all minimum payment amounts, and the rest goes into Debt 1 until it is completely paid off. Move to the next debt until that one is paid off, and so forth.

The second method to tackling this debt is the *Math Teacher Method*. The reason I call it the *Math Teacher Method* is because you do more math and calculating to save the most amount of money. If you get this method right, you will save a lot of money. I will admit I personally followed this method and a little bit of the Debt Snowball. What attracted me to this method is that you pay off your debts by highest interest rate first and work your way down to the lowest interest rate. If you have a 25 percent interest APR credit card hanging out there plus a 2 percent auto loan, but you opt to go with the Debt Snowball method instead, you risk incurring a lot more interest had you just paid off the high interest credit card first and then the auto loan. Basically, input all your debts again, but this time in the order of high interest rate to low interest. Pay the minimum payments first on all the debts, but whatever cash you have left over after your budget, throw that at the high interest rate loan first and work your way down to the smallest. This will allow you to save hundreds, if not thousands, of dollars on interest accrued.

The con to this method is you won't have the instant gratification that you will receive in the Debt Snowball. Furthermore, if you have debts with similar interest rates like 2.9 percent and 3.5 percent, obviously there isn't much to lose, so I would revert to the Debt Snowball if you fall in to that scenario. Again, don't spend too much time agonizing over numbers and stats for how the debt is going be cleared; just list it, organize it, and make it happen.

The *Math Teacher* debt payment strategy should look similar to this:
Debt 1: $4,500 (Minimum Payment $50/Month with an interest rate 30 percent)
Debt 2: $3,000 (Minimum Payment $150/Month with an interest rate of 18 percent)
Debt 3: $750 (Minimum Payment $35/Month with an interest rate of 10 percent)
Debt 4: $8,000 (Minimum Payment $100/Month with an interest rate of 2 percent)

Leftover cash from your budget in Chapter 1 goes toward all minimum payments, and the rest goes into *Debt 1* until it is paid in full. Once Debt 1 is paid in full, you will then allocate all your *Leftover cash* to Debt 2 while paying the minimum payments on the remaining debts. Repeat this strategy until all debts have been eliminated.

The third method is the *Avoidance Method*. I recommend it almost never—only in special circumstances if my client is overwhelmed with debt, possesses a lot of debts that are high interest, and they need a more straightforward system to pay off what they owe. The reason it is called the *Avoidance Method* is because what we essentially do in this method is consolidate all of our debts into one large loan at a lower interest rate; sometimes it can be higher if not done correctly. You can find these loans through your credit card company, bank, or credit union.

You apply for the loan, and when you're approved, they will mail a blank check to write out to yourself to deposit in your bank account. Once the funds are available in your account, you can start issuing payments to lenders you owe. Some banks will send the payment to the lenders you owe directly once you are approved, so be sure to have those account numbers handy, along with the exact payoff amount for those loans.

After consolidating, we get this illusion of temporary gratification and completion. The reason this method should be approached with caution is because most of us, if not all, will have that great feeling of accomplishment and start to believe we solved our debt problem. We start to just make the minimum payments, or in some cases don't pay at all because the minimum payment is too large to fit in our budget. After months have passed, we come back to reality and realize the problem is still there and we have accomplished absolutely nothing. As I mentioned earlier, this a marathon. Be careful of those quick wins that may seem like you solved the issue, but all you did was put a Band-Aid on it. If you do decide to go this route, make sure you do a gut check, and be 100 percent sure you will stay the course no matter how low the payment is, or how long the bank stretched the loan for. I particularly don't like this method, but as I stated earlier, I give a little leeway under special circumstances, as everyone's battle is different.

Double Check Your Work

Next, after you have chosen the method that you're most comfortable with and one that applies to your personal financial situation, observe the debts and make sure the amounts are truly what you owe. Sometimes lenders slide in fees, or collection agencies add extra costs to servicing the bill. Make sure you are being billed what you truly owe. Don't just pay because they sent a letter demanding that you pay.

Once you are 100 percent sure of the balances you owe, research to see the types of loans you have. Some auto loans are simple interest loans (these use the current amount outstanding the day of the principal balance), and some are precomputed (these use the total principal and interest of the entire loan in advance to determine the balance due). If you fall into a situation where they don't allow you to pay to principal only, you may have to refinance out of the loan with a lender that will allow principal-only payments. Be sure to read your loan contract for more information. If you have bad credit, can't refinance, and your lender won't allow principal payments, pay the normal amount and save everything extra you were going to pay toward it. Once you have the full loan amount saved, pay them off in one swoop.

Some loans/credit cards have extremely high interest rates of 20 percent or higher. If possible, look into transferring balances to a 0 percent interest card or a low-interest personal loan to relieve yourself of the high interest. Nevertheless, don't do this to every single loan with a high interest and balance (for example, you don't need to do this for a balance of, say, only $200). If you have a balance of $10,000, then yes, that would be a good scenario to just refinance out. But again, everyone's situation is different. If you make $100,000 a year and have a $10,000 high-interest loan, you can pay that off in a month or two. If your income is $20,000 a year and you owe $10,000 with a high interest, then yes, refinancing may be more economical.

Pay What You Owe - Collections
Another area for concern that most people have is how to handle collections. There are tons of resources online that show highly effective ways to get rid of collections and horrible, inefficient ways to stay in debt to collectors. Most collections fall off your credit report after seven years. This is not a guarantee, but the statute of limitations in most states mandate that collections can only be reported up to seven years. They can reappear on your credit report after the seven years if they are persistent and eventually sell the debt to another collection agency. Occasionally, they summon you to appear in court or slap judgements against you to garnish your wages. My basic rule for handling

collectors is broken down into four words I used at the beginning of this chapter: *Pay What You Owe.*

You are not responsible for the ridiculous fees that are added on to the collection bills, but I will hold you responsible for paying the balance that you originally owed. If you are in extreme poverty and simply cannot afford these bills, then I understand. Offer whatever you can afford to give to settle the debt. If it is not enough to settle, don't worry about the collectors. Address them later when you can settle for a reasonable amount. When you settle the debt, be sure to get the settlement in writing and pay them with a money order, check, or method that doesn't give them access to your credit card or bank account to withdraw whatever amount they want. Occasionally, the collection agency will withdraw the entire collection bill from the bank account once you provide them your account information.

If you have the income to afford the debt, only pay them the original balance that you owed or less. Sometimes you can negotiate the debt down over 50 percent to settle at an amount that won't break your bank account. Get the settlement in writing and pay with a money order, check, prepaid card, etc. As I stated earlier, if you are in poverty, do not worry about these collectors until you are back on your feet and can afford to pay them off.

As you get out debt, you want to continue to search for ways to increase your income so that you can pay remaining debt down faster. What's better than getting out of debt? Getting out of debt quickly, and with a higher paycheck.

The importance of getting out of debt in Step 3 is that we don't want to move forward into our future with obligations that suck our income stream dry. What's the purpose of working all those long hours only to see the money disappear to some lender or bank that you owe?

Think of debt as being a prisoner for a certain amount of time, forced into free labor, minimal pleasure, and being trapped 24/7. I know it's not a happy image, but you need to harden your mindset now that you've decided to free yourself from the chains of debt. I apologize for such a harsh example, but I want everyone to understand the seriousness and repercussions of going into tremendous debt. There isn't a such thing as good debt and bad debt; all debt is bad, because at the end of the day, you are a slave to the person/entity whom you owe.

Follow Your Mentors, Follow Your Dream
I am a huge Robert Kiyosaki fan, and love his book *Rich Dad Poor Dad*. As a matter of fact, he is one of the top mentors I listen to for real estate and investing advice. Though his strategies made him very successful, I always advise people to never feel as though they have to pick one extreme over the other. Sometimes everything one expert teaches isn't for everybody. Even the getting-out-of-debt strategies within this book won't benefit a billionaire who uses debt to operate their business.

Every person is different mentally, physically, and spiritually. One expert's advice may make one person extremely successful if done correctly while causing another person, who may not have done thorough research, to fail miserably. One could buy a lot of real estate incorrectly and go into debt only to find out later that they didn't properly vet the investments and could be headed into bankruptcy. That's why it's important to find experts who speak to your personal financial situation.

For example, a person who is a beginner at real-estate investing should follow the Dave Ramsey approach of paying cash for real-estate investments. When you pay cash, you are reducing risk and insuring yourself against foreclosure. Why do banks force customers to buy private mortgage insurance when they put down less than 20%? Because they have to protect themselves in case you fail.

On the other side of the isle, if you are very creative, do the research and invest the good debt strategically, you should follow the Robert Kiyosaki approach. When you have experience and research under your belt, you are less of a risk to the bank and yourself.

I personally prefer to pay cash. However, if the investment deal checks out, I may take out a small amount debt to finance the property only to pay it off as fast as possible.

Overall, you get the picture. I would not recommend going in to debt for a Ferrari, but if you have done the proper research, it's OK to take on debt to invest in income producing assets such as real estate.

I remember as a kid working alongside my grandparents, who invested in real estate. I witnessed the pros and cons of owning rentals, and the many challenges you face dealing with tenants. However, I truly believe if you develop a good system and team, you could have a sustainable and cost-effective operation.

The reason I haven't taken the dive into real estate yet is because I'm saving up the cash to buy my first property outright or put more than 20 percent down. Some disagree, but who cares. I'm still young, so why rush to go into mortgage debt?

Final Thoughts on the Chapter

As I stated earlier in the Rainy Day step, continue to invest in your retirement accounts up to your employer's match. If your employer doesn't offer a match, invest a very conservative amount of your income so that you don't miss out on the compounding effect of time and investing. A very conservative amount could be 1 to 5 percent of your income. Depending on your overall debt load, you may not be able to invest entirely, so don't worry about investing for retirement until you are debt free or have significantly reduced the total amount you owe. Paying off debt is still an investment because you are saving on the interest of loan, which is a guaranteed return on investment, or ROI.

And remember, after paying off credit cards, do not close the account unless it charges you an annual fee. Closing all of your accounts will cause your credit score to drop and will leave you with zero credit history.

Lots of information covered so far, so feel free to glance back through the chapter for details on what strategies that may fit your situation to get out of debt quickly and efficiently.

Overall, get out debt, stay out of debt, set yourself free, and let the wealth building begin!

Chapter 4: Stormy Day/Emergency Fund

Congratulations if you have completed Steps 1 through 3 and you are finally debt free! Being debt free should be celebrated as a huge milestone in your life as big as our golden birthdays or wedding anniversaries. Yes, it's that serious. Often, in a privileged country, we tend to prioritize moments/accomplishments that were passed down or advertised to us via the media or by our parents. That is not to discount graduating high school or meeting the love of your life. However, what would our lives look like if we were chained to debt for ten, twenty, forty or more years of our life until we pass on? How do we secure the financial foundation of our loved ones if we are no longer present or able to produce income? How do we retire from a taxing work life without any funds to take care of ourself and our spouse? I have seen very ugly scenarios that people live out to this present day, all in the name of debt. So, celebrate this moment, capture it for your loved ones to see, remember it, and let it be a priority over the irrelevant things of life. Now, we are not finished with our financial steps to freedom, but I don't want this moment to go unrecognized. The day you became debt free is the day you became a free person. I became debt free April 30, 2017, and I will always remember it. Very important that you remind yourself of this moment and remind your children, if you have any, of what it takes and what it feels like to no longer be trapped under the suffocating crush of debt.

I truly have to celebrate you in this great moment of your life, and you owe it to yourself to do the same. Now, we aren't going on a month-long vacation to Hawaii just yet. We have PLENTY of work to do to achieve our financial goals.

This brings us to our Stormy Day/Life Emergency Fund. In Step 2, I recommended you start a Rainy Day Fund. At that point in time, we wanted to develop enough cash to take care of temporary inconveniences and so-called rainy days that occurred during this process.

I call this the Stormy Day Fund because you will need more than just an umbrella for these time periods of your life. This fund will be added on top of your initial partial savings fund, meaning you should already have at least one-month's-worth of savings. I highly recommend putting back, at the very least, three months' emergency savings to a generous twelve months' emergency savings. If you wish to become even more secure, twenty-four months of savings is also a good option.

Once you start to save an additional three to twenty-four months' expenses on top of the initial emergency savings, it is important to remember to pick an amount that will make you more comfortable during times of job loss, hardship, or health issues that delay your ability to produce income.

Possibly, more than twelve months' savings is beneficial in cases where you can't obtain life insurance, you are self-employed, or the nature of your employment is similar to contract work that has very large gaps of unproductive time. I am not recommending more than twenty-four months max, but it's an option if your situation calls for it. I personally opted for twelve months' savings because that's what makes me comfortable at night when I sleep. You could very much be comfortable with three months and not blink an eye.

Think you don't need this extended-purpose fund? Think again. According to the Bureau of Labor Statistics (BLS), during economic downturns or after a sudden job loss, the average person stayed unemployed anywhere between three and six months. During 2010, in the depths of the so-called Great Recession, the BLS states, the average person needed almost half a year to regain employment. That's bad enough, but how much more difficult was it for those unemployed Americans who also suffered injuries, accidents, or other traumatic life events at their time of greatest need? Life happens, and what you think can never happen to you could be as close as the next recession. Because of all of this, you need to think long and hard about these emergency funds. Your health and welfare, as well as that of your family and loved ones, could very well depend on your expert planning.

I will say that you should make sure when calculating your Stormy Day Fund to think of every possible thing that could go wrong. If applicable, add your spouse into the equation as well. That is not to promote grim and pessimistic thinking, but we live in a real world where real situations and circumstance apply. Those who prepare for the future will control their family's future, and those who don't prepare will be the ones being controlled by external powers/entities. I repeat, I am not trying to be negative or take jabs at anyone. I just want there to be a clear understanding that life happens to everyone at unpredictable times.

Once the amount has been set for your Stormy Day Fund, it is time to hit the ground running once again with the same intensity as you displayed getting out of debt. That's why it's important not to party too hard when you get out of debt because you are going to want to relax. But the battle goes on.

Super Saving

A few options to achieve this goal in a reasonable time frame are to sell more things around the house that you no longer need, work overtime at your place of employment, drive for Uber, or many other opportunities that are available at your fingertips. This is very similar to Step 1, when I provided you with a few ways to fund your savings. Reapply those methods to this step, and you will have a fully funded account in no time. Also, think of saving into a Stormy Day Fund this way. Before, you were living paycheck to paycheck, meaning you spent as much as you earned. Now that you are out of debt, you should have money left over that you were originally putting toward debt payments. This could have been 10, 20, or even 50 percent of your income going to debt obligations. This is no longer the circumstance, and now you have that same amount available to deposit straight into your savings account.

First, I recommend setting up direct deposit to your savings account so that every time you get paid, the money hits your account directly. Allocate the entire amount you were using for debt into savings. If you received a promotion or increase in pay, adjust, and contribute that extra amount to savings, as well.

For every 50 percent of income you save from each check, it is one month's worth of savings. I may have just blown your mind away for a second, but it is completely true!

Think of it this way. If you only need 50 percent of your income to take care of all of your expenses for that month, that means the 50 percent you just saved will take care of you for one month in the future. This is a very efficient system, and it is proven. I push myself to live off 40 to 50 percent of my income, allowing me to save/invest the rest every pay period. When I get married, hopefully, we will be able to live off 50 percent of my income, save the other 50 percent and save my wife's entire paycheck if she decides to work. So, for those of you who are married, you can push to save one spouse's check, and use the other to pay for living expenses. Or minimize down to almost half of one spouse's check and save 75 percent of your total household income.

I have spoken with plenty of married couples who use that system of saving one spouse's check and using the other for expenses. In all cases, it works, and they love it. Some even opt to have one parent stay at home with the children because they figured it to be efficient and more cost-effective if they pocket daycare/education costs.

Additionally, once you have set up direct deposit, you can seek other ways to fund the Stormy Day Fund. Remember, there are more steps ahead in order to be financially free, so we still want to complete this step fairly quickly. After you have obtained six months' worth of expenses, please continue to the next step, which is retirement planning. You will continue to work toward your goal of a fully funded account if you want to have more than six months' worth of savings, for example, but you will do so while saving for retirement. This prevents you from missing out on the time and compounding effect of investing early. If you only want six months' worth of savings, then you are completely done with this step.

An important strategy to consider after completing your Stormy Day Fund is to continue to allocate a small percentage of your income to be deposited into this account each month. Could be $20, or it could $150 a month. The idea is to keep increasing your savings so that as small emergencies, or inconvenient purchases, arise, you rarely hit your principal emergency fund amount. For example: If you save $20,000 in your Stormy Day Fund and contribute an extra $20/month, in six months you will have $120 extra on top of your emergency savings. If the battery goes out on your car or you have to make a quick $100 repair, you can use that $120 part of your Stormy Day Fund to pay for the inconvenience—without touching your initial amount.

You can also divvy up your emergency savings into categories such as vacation fund, car repair fund, doctor visit fund, etc. These are just examples, but definitely make it easy to save up for those other big purchases that may not rise to the level of an emergency. Now, don't divide up the actual emergency fund, just have separate categories of accounts that you save on top of your emergency fund to organize and plan for those future purchases.

When SHTF!
This next part of the Stormy Day Fund plan is completely, 100 percent optional. It will not affect your financially free journey negatively if you decide not to implement this step, so feel free to skip ahead to the retirement-planning chapter.

I want to include it in this process because it is important to be ready financially; however, it also important to be prepared physically. Therefore, I recommend, as an additional precaution, that you buy or make a bugout bag/emergency kit. Coupled with other disaster preparedness items, this will come in handy and possibly save you and your family's lives in emergencies. Some of you may have watched the TV series 'Doomsday Preppers' and can relate this step to that show, but this is more of a basic approach for the average person who may not have as much knowledge as a professional prepper. You can buy preassembled kits online anywhere from $75 to $1,000, depending on how many supplies are in each kit and the brand you prefer.

I have read numerous articles about situations where people were caught in natural disasters and lacked something as basic as water. Some people that were prepared were able to survive those additional days because they prepped and had enough food until emergency assistance arrived. So, it may not be the end of the world, but anything can happen in your region that would cause you to rely on your emergency kit to survive. Hurricanes, tornadoes, earthquakes, tsunamis, violent protests, floods, etc., are all things that have happened and can happen again, even in America. In some areas, people can't even breathe the air after some chemical plant explodes. I know this has absolutely nothing to do with finance, but a debit card and cash won't be able to feed, hydrate, or save you in a severe disaster. God forbid the worst happens to anyone, but I always advise clients to stay ready, so you don't have to *get* ready. If you are already well versed and prepared for a disaster, you can skip the panic part and go straight to executing your disaster preparedness plan.

Many friends and clients ask, "Dan, what does your emergency plan look like?" To briefly answer, I always keep extra water in the house in addition to water for daily use. Also, I shop in bulk, which leaves me with extra food and other goods every day no matter if I use them. I have a "bugout bag" for each person in my family that can carry food, medical supplies, a flashlight, batteries, a knife, a radio, any many other items that we may need if we decide to leave our home on foot.

Firearms and training are also part of my emergency plan. I go to the gun range twice a month to sharpen my skills so that I am always prepared and ready to protect my family. Some firearms training experts recommend training under high stress and in different firing positions. This will create a more realistic feeling when you are in danger and under stress, and your training will kick in. Always check with your local range or training facility for their rules and attend their classes, if offered.

Some people may even take offense to this concept, but the reality is that criminals do not care about the law or whether guns are illegal. A criminal is always on the search for an easy target that displays the least resistance. If you don't like the idea of guns, consider taking other self-defense classes and buying a Taser.

Exercising daily and maintaining a healthy diet is also part of my emergency plan, as this increases your chance of survival if you need to run or carry your gear. Who wants to have all the resources they need to survive an emergency but can't walk one mile? It is important to have a healthy diet and stay in shape so your body can function under the least ideal situations.

Now, what do you do financially—you know—if the economy collapses? Financially, I continue both to invest in the stock market and to save for real estate, but if the entire economy or government falls, my 401(k) will not save me. So, I purchased some silver and gold to barter in situations where I might need to make trades or purchases. Consider adding precious metals to your portfolio; about 5 percent or less than $10,000 is a good amount. For those who may not be able to buy lump sums of silver, you can try finding quarters that were minted before 1964; these were made of silver.

Finally, I try to network with other like-minded individuals who are preppers as well. This is a huge community, and many people are willing to help and provide tips/guidance on best practices.

Chapter 5: Building Credit the Right Way

I created this chapter to discuss credit building because what I have witnessed over the years as a financial coach is that many people have the idea of credit misconstrued. Some people believe that simply paying the electric bill builds up credit, while others thought they were building credit by paying their phone bill on time. Both concepts are completely untrue. I will debunk all of these myths and instill facts on how to properly build your credit. So, let's get started.

At this point in the process, you should be out of debt and have a fully funded emergency fund. Having these two accomplishments under your belt is the start to a secure financial foundation. We don't want to take steps back into debt, but rather we want to understand debt and how credit can be used to benefit you. There are even ways to have good credit without debt.

Some financial experts promote not obtaining any credit period, which is very wise. Granted, having good credit basically means you are good at borrowing money and paying it back on time. It also means that you can borrow more money in the future at a potentially low interest rate. From that standpoint, there isn't a point in having good credit if you plan to just borrow more money and end up in debt again.

Even though there are plenty of reasons to not have a credit, I continuously receive inquiries from clients insisting that I teach them how to build credit. Moreover, it is possible to have good credit without taking on any debt. You can even use credit temporarily to earn cash back and save on certain purchases without going deeply into debt.

As I stated in previous chapters, debt is the enemy and should be avoided at all costs. I stand by that statement. However, I understand that having good credit is becoming more apparent in our daily lives, which is why I decided to assist by dedicating an entire chapter to how to build credit the right way.

Credit is a very interesting topic that has left many people confused and often scared to deal with. This is not surprising because it seems like the banks that issue these cards make it as difficult as possible to understand the terms of your credit agreement. Still, having a healthy credit history is not only important for buying a home, but it is also starting to become part of the background check process when seeking employment. My goal at the end of this chapter is to provide you with the tools and knowledge necessary to help you achieve a healthy credit profile— without taking on massive debt to get there.

Discipline

As a good rule of thumb, one way to determine if you should proceed through this chapter to learn about building credit is to ask yourself one question. "Do I have self-discipline?" If the answer is yes, you can start to learn how to build credit. If the answer is no, I don't recommend you focus on building credit—at least for now.

If you don't know the answer, take a quick look at your life. Are you organized? Do you have a consistent schedule that you adhere to most of the time? When you go shopping, do you stick to your budget, or do you impulsively spend on items you don't need?

These are important questions because part of building credit is responsibility and self-discipline. If you answered no to any of those questions above, my recommendation is to wait until the very end of this process, reevaluate your self-discipline, and proceed from there. Hopefully, by the end you won't need credit at all.

The most common way to determine your credit health is by viewing your credit score. When we think of our credit score, the first thing we commonly think of is credit cards. Yes, credit cards do affect your credit report and credit score, but so do many other lines of credit such as personal loans, student loans, and auto loans.

You can think of your credit score as a trust score; can we (the lending institution) trust you (the borrower) to use this money responsibly and pay us back in a timely manner while adhering to our contract/agreement?

Since the 1950s, credit cards have taken the world by storm, with 24/7 access to credit, reward points, international spending ability, and approval decisions within seconds. Credit cards are the most common way to establish credit history, build credit, and make purchases securely without having to worry about fraud that could drain your entire checking account if you use a debit card.

With all this power however, does come great responsibility. If you are late on payments, use over 30 percent of your credit limit/exceed your limit, or misuse your credit card to make unnecessary purchases, you will more than likely find yourself in extreme debt, with a very low credit score, and unable to apply for additional credit in the future.

The Five Factors

There are five factors that significantly affect your credit score: on-time payments, credit utilization, length of credit history, types of credit, and inquiries/new credit.

First up, on-time payments. As stated earlier, lending institutions want to see if they can trust you as a borrower, thus they check your credit score. Your payment history affects a whopping 35 percent of your credit score, which is why this is the most important factor to remember. If you are struggling with building credit, the most basic thing you can do today is pay the balance due on time every month. As months and years pass, you can either build good history by paying on time, or bad history by missing payments and being late.

Credit utilization affects a total of 30 percent of your score. Think about the amount of credit you currently have access to, whether it's $1,000 or $20,000. When you use your credit card or other lines of revolving credit, part of your score is determined by the amount you owe and the amount available to you. Most credit experts advise people to stay under 30 percent, meaning if you have a total $1,000 available to you, then it is best to spend no more than $300. In contrast, I typically recommend clients use credit as sparingly as possible, possibly on utility bills or other mandatory living expenses. Moreover, I advise everyone to pay off their credit cards in full each time they use them.

Many other types of loan balances such as your auto, student, and personal loans can affect this portion of your report as well, depending on if you paid a large portion of the balance down or if you are barely keeping up. For example, if you took out an auto loan in 2013 for $20,000 and in 2018 the balance is $5,000, this shows credit agencies that you are responsible and can pay off loans in a timely manner.

Next, length of credit history. Establishing an extensive, on-time payment history reveals to creditors your consistency and reliability when it comes to paying your loans. This portion of your credit affects 15 percent of your score and sort of goes hand-in-hand with payment history.

One of the biggest ways to contribute positively to this part of your credit score is to start building credit as early as possible. After opening your first credit card account at age twenty-one, for example, leaving it open until you are thirty-one is ten years of credit history! Now, other factors such as new lines of credit can affect your history because the credit bureaus calculate the "average" length of all of your accounts.

It is important to remember that when paying off debt, it is OK to leave open credit card accounts after you have paid them in full. The only time I recommend closing them is if they charge a significant annual fee. Closing these accounts will eliminate that history and reflect negatively in your credit score.

In addition to those previous factors, another credit factor is types of credit. As we work down the list, the credit score factors to follow will have less effect on your score. One of them is having different types of credit and diversifying your credit mix. This factor has a 10 percent impact on your score.

I don't recommend focusing on obtaining different types of credit because it has a low impact on your score, and as you go into more debt you open yourself up to more risk. I do recommend having a credit card, but it is not mandatory to go obtain an auto loan, personal line of credit, or student loan to increase your credit mix. Moreover, when you do get a credit card, I only advise you to use it for basic necessities, as stated earlier, and pay it off every month in full.

 Lastly, inquiries/new credit. The last and final factor is new credit/inquires, which only affects 10 percent of your score. Inquiries occur when an individual or a lending intuition reviews your credit report with the bureau at which they are inquiring (Equifax, Transunion, or Experian). When you are approved for a loan or line of credit, this is now listed as new credit. If you have obtained more than one to three new lines of credit recently, most creditors will not approve you for any more due to the increased risk.

Review Your Credit Report Once a Month!

While you monitor your credit and seek ways to increase your score, it is also a good idea to review your report with all three bureaus for any errors or suspicious activity. Look for accounts that you don't recognize or inquiries that you didn't authorize. This will prevent you from becoming a victim of identity theft and fraud.

Furthermore, make it a monthly ritual to browse every line of your credit report to make sure everything is correct.

I recall a time I applied for credit at an auto dealership, and they sent my information to ten banks and all ten left an inquiry on my credit report. Completely unethical and shouldn't have been done, but if I hadn't checked my credit report, I wouldn't have known they did that.

Credit is a partial indicator of your overall financial health, and in the eyes of other banks, those ten inquires made me look very irresponsible and desperate. So, hold yourself accountable to check your report each month. There are plenty of companies such as Credit Karma and some credit card issuers that provide you with a monthly credit report from certain credit agencies.

This is all brings back memories of how my credit journey started. My first experience with credit was when I was eighteen years old and was approved for my first credit card with a line of credit totaling a whopping $500. Prior to that, I was denied credit many times by Chase, Discover, and American Express. At the time, I didn't know that those were the most prestigious banks to have a credit card and I would need a little more credit history in order to be approved by them.

The bank that approved me for my first card was called Southern Bancorp. It was a local bank I was using at the time, and they happily gave me a shot to prove my credit worthiness. The interest rate was egregious—a crazy 25 percent. Luckily, I was very tempered and used my card to pay for necessities such as my cell phone bill and quickly paid it off before the statement balance was due.

Watch Out for the Traps

After I discovered credit and started increasing my credit score, I fell in love with the thought of borrowing money now to pay back later. As my score increased, I started to receive lower interest rates and more credit offers. I think you can see where this is going.

Once I thought I had become a master of credit, I started to make larger purchases. I bought a 2012 Dodge Charger, then traded it in and bought a 2013 Dodge Challenger. After the Challenger, I bought a 2009 Ninja 650 motorcycle and then purchased a 2014 Dodge Charger. I was dissatisfied with the standard equipment and started to upgrade the sound systems, monitors, and wheels, all purchased with credit.

Furthermore, during this same time period, I was a full-time college student, a single dad, and an employee. Thus, leading me to take out student loans because I couldn't "afford" tuition.

I continued to pay my credit card bills on time and auto loans, but as you can see, I created a cycle for myself. Borrow, buy, pay back, and repeat. All of this led me to live paycheck to paycheck.

There were two turning points in my life that changed my outlook on finance forever. The time I had to spend $10,000 in a custody battle for my son, and the day I was denied credit to buy my first home/investment property. These events changed my financial life forever.

When I was denied for the mortgage loan, my net worth was outlined on the loan documents as negative $65,000.

So, this is why credit is bad. This is why debt should be avoided. If I had followed the steps outlined in this text, maybe the outcome for me would have been different. I would have been able to cash flow the custody case and own my first piece of real estate at age twenty-one.

To this day, I sparingly use credit, and the only types of credit I use are credit cards/lines of credit. This is my recommendation to you if you possess the first characteristic I outlined earlier in this chapter—self-discipline.

The reason I recommend only opening a credit card is because it is the easiest and least harmful method to build credit if you use it wisely. All you have to do is apply for one, use it sparingly for necessities, pay it off in full each month, and leave the account open forever. If you already have one, just make sure to pay it off, and leave the account active.

Again, the only time I recommend closing a credit card is if it charges a high annual fee just for having the card, the company has a history of fraud/hacking, or if you can't simply control your spending. Other than that, it's perfectly fine to possess a credit card.

First Approvals are Often the Hardest

If you lack any credit at all and have a hard time getting approved for your first credit card, there three things you can do. You can try a local bank/credit union that you are member of and ask for a credit card or line of credit through them. Usually, they will take into consideration your banking history with them and may offer you a small amount of credit to start with. This is how I got approved for my first credit card.

Maybe you don't have a good history with the bank, and they deny you. You can apply for a secured credit card that you have to deposit the funds into in order to start using it. Think of it as the bank's way of protecting itself if you fail to pay the credit card off. I have seen people that were able to deposit as little as $500 get started with one of these cards. The only downside to some of these accounts is the bank that approves you sometimes charges an annual fee.

If those options don't pan out, there are credit-builder loans you can take out that require you to pay a fee and deposit the funds upfront to pay back over a selected period of time. A way to think of these loan products is a form of self-lending. You are basically borrowing money from yourself and paying yourself back that same amount of money over a certain period of time. Depending on how bad your credit is, a year or two is good length of time to pay back these loans to allow your credit history to be built. If paid on time each month, you will create a good credit history that will allow you to apply for a regular credit card in the future.

Once you build up enough credit history with the secured card or credit-builder loan, you can attempt to obtain an unsecured credit card either through that same institution or a different one. A good amount of time to wait is one year before attempting to apply for an unsecured card if you start with the secured credit card. If you go with the credit-builder loan, just wait until you have completed paying back the loan in full.

While using any of those strategies, do not attempt to apply for any more credit or have anyone inquire about your credit report. This will reduce your credit score further, especially if more than three exist on your report already. Many creditors deny you credit for simply having too many inquiries within a short time period.

If you are unsure if someone is going to run your credit report or inquire, just ask. There are numerous times someone thought I authorized them to check my credit because most people just go with the flow and allow it. But I always ask them if they need to check my credit, and if the answer is yes, I tell them not to. If they say it's required for whatever they are trying to do, I deny the service if it's not important.

Another easy way to build credit if you have a tough time getting approved for your first card is to ask a relative or your significant other to add you as an authorized user on their credit card account. This will automatically allow you to start building history and your credit score. The only downside to this option is you have to make sure they are responsible users of credit. It will not benefit you if they are irresponsible and miss payments. This further decreases your chances of getting approved for a credit card, so be careful when going this route.

If you are uncomfortable relying on them to pay the card off each month, you can ask them to cosign on a credit card with you so that you are in control. Again, the risk is still high because if you don't pay the card on time, you risk ruining their credit, as well.

But these two latter options (Authorized user/Co-signer) should only be considered if you have exhausted all other methods and desperately need to start building your credit. I don't recommend it as a first resort. With great discretion, only limit these strategies to your spouse, children, or direct family members. Even then, be very careful because you don't want to ruin any relationships within the family. And nothing will ruin a relationship faster than a problem with money.

Keep it Simple

After you have you first card, as I stated, only use it for items you need, and pay it off in full every month. Do not use it to finance a TV, phone, or car! Leave it active for as long as you can, and you will see your credit history increase each year.

A good number of cards can range anywhere from three to six. I personally have over twenty, but that is only because I use different benefits that each card offers, and I sort of have an addiction to credit card churning (Credit card churning is the use of credit cards to gain cash back and reward points).

Some may ask, should I take out an auto loan, student loan, or other different types of credit to diversify my credit types? The short answer, and what I recommend, is no. You don't need all of those different credit types to have good credit. They may help increase your score faster, but it is not worth it. Stick to only the credit cards and a mortgage if you wish to finance your home. I even promote paying cash for your home if you can, but not everyone can do that.

Now, you can do what you feel is best for your situation, and you may very well opt to finance your car, for instance, so that you can keep your cash in your bank account. Nothing is wrong with that, and I will not argue against that. The fact that you have the cash in the bank to pay for the car in full tells me you are disciplined and will have no issue paying the auto loan back. But if you are a person living paycheck to paycheck like I was, I am 100 percent against taking out any loans.

Additionally, just remember to keep things simple. We only need good credit if we are trying to get a mortgage or to borrow money at a low interest rate. To be more specific, we only want to use our good credit score to obtain debt strategically so that it can be used as a means to an end. From my experience, any score above 700 will do the job for you. You can easily get there without using large loans, and only using your credit cards and paying them off on time.

Not only do banks look at your score, but they also look at your debt-to-income ratio to see how much debt you have. This is where those student loans and auto loans can work against you. Yes, they help mix up your debt types and marginally increase your credit score, but they hurt you when trying to obtain a mortgage or other larger loans.

For those that may be wondering what your debt-to-income ratio is, it's a formula banks use to see what percentage of your income is being used to pay off debt. You can calculate this by first adding all of your minimum monthly debt payments together. Then divide that total amount by your monthly gross income. This will give you a percentage, which is your debt-to-income ratio, or DTI. For example, if you're your credit card payments, auto loans, and other debt obligations equal $1,000 and your total monthly gross income is $2,000, your DTI is 50 percent. Fifty percent is considered very high, and you will more than likely be denied the mortgage.

Overall, building credit doesn't have to be difficult or require some complex strategy. If you do as I outlined in this chapter and only use a credit card to build your credit score, you will be perfectly fine and reach the 700 club.

In the previous steps of the financial longevity journey, I asked you to pay off all debt except for the mortgage. If you followed that advice and reached this point of being debt free, you should see an increase in your credit score automatically.

To summarize my recommendations to building credit: obtain a credit card if you don't already have one, use it for necessities, pay it off in full each month before the interest kicks in, and repeat. Nothing more, nothing less. If you can get one to three cards in that same year, that works, as well. That strategy will maximize your overall credit limit, which will help increase your score.

After achieving a good credit score, you will gradually see positive changes in your finances. To name a few, your auto insurance premium may drop because insurance companies like to use your credit reports to evaluate your risk. You may find that you are able to get certain jobs such as a police officer, accountant, financial coach, bank manager, etc., because typically these jobs require applicants to have a good credit history and display a history of financial responsibility. At some apartment complexes, you won't be required to put down a deposit or extra month's rent due to having a good credit history. If you decide to take a loan out on a car (I hope you don't do this), you will be able to lock in a very low interest rate.

You will have access to low-interest credit to start or expand a business endeavor. The endless positive benefits for having great credit go on and on.

My personal favorite of them all is credit card churning, which is basically using your credit cards solely for sign-up bonuses and reward points. Each year, I rack up thousands of dollars' worth of rewards and sign-up bonuses, which really come in handy when you want to stretch your dollars. For example, you may do a lot shopping for groceries each year that equates to $5000, and the card you use offers a 5% cash back option. This will allow you to receive a check for $250 that you can use for anything you want! Quite the strategy, if you ask me!

As you go through this credit-building journey, it important to note that credit is a game of patience. The more good history you create, the higher your score will be. Don't rush trying to apply for every single credit card and signing your name to auto loans; just be patient with what you have. Slow and steady wins the race.

Chapter 6: Higher Education and Employment

For those who may be younger and just starting their adult life, I wanted to dedicate a chapter to what to expect now that you are about to enter adulthood. If you are an older adult and looking to hit the reset button in pursuit of higher education and better employment opportunities, this chapter will benefit you, as well.

The moment you graduate high school, you will have to decide whether or not to pursue a college degree or certificate. Many of you will have to start searching for employment opportunities. If you are hardheaded like I was, you may find yourself doing both while raising a newborn child. That is not to frown upon those who have children at a young age, but let's be honest: It's not a good idea to have children while you are unemployed and can barely take care of yourself. Please pay heed to what I'm saying, and don't have children before marriage. Wait until you live your life, get married later, create a solid foundation where one spouse has the choice to stay home, and let it be planned. Too many people like me prematurely have kids—before we get rid of our own inner kid. There isn't a reason to rush; trust and believe me. When your child is born, you die. To give better context into that statement, all of your dreams, ambitions, and pleasures take the backseat until you successfully raise your child into a productive adult.

I don't want to turn this into a lecture, but I want to create a guide for those that may find themselves lost during these important early years of your life. It's completely normal to admit you're lost. Usually, the problem arises when you think that you are not lost and that you know everything there is to know about life. Parents can sometimes sound like a beating drum; nevertheless, they naturally want what's best for you so that you enter the world with plenty of opportunities. If anyone knows about how precious time is, it's going to be your parents, grandparents, guardian, or someone that is older than you. James 1:19 states, "Everyone should be quick to listen, slow to speak, and slow to become angry." This means shut up if someone is trying to give you wisdom about something you don't know and they have a proven track record of success.

First topic, higher education. As a society, we have created this narrative that every single child should pursue a college degree in any field of study that they have a "passion" for. We also have promoted a failed strategy of lending eighteen-year-olds thousands, if not hundreds of thousands of dollars in student loans. This has resulted in what financial experts call a student loan bubble. Whether you believe it's happening or not, it is 100 percent true that we as a nation have a student loan epidemic. As I write this section of the book in the year 2018, the national student loan debt has recently surpassed $1.5 trillion, according to USDebtClock.org.

I wouldn't say that I or any other student is a victim of student loan debt, but I will say that I was misled into thinking student loans were harmless and just a normal part of life. This perception has led millions of young adults into a lifelong debt trap. This trend only gets worse for minorities. In fact, nearly half of all black students who enrolled in 2003-2004 defaulted on at least one loan over the next twelve years, compared with one in five white students over the same time period, according to an analysis by Robert Kelchen, assistant professor of higher education at Seton Hall University. This growing problem affects all racial groups.

It is my hope to prevent you from making these mistakes and forgo taking out any debt.

If you are contemplating going to college, you will first have to determine the costs and expected job growth and salary in your field of study. It is critical that you conduct this research prior to enrolling. Some colleges tell you to visit academic advisers, but they work for the school, so what do you expect them to tell you? Do your own due diligence. You are an adult now, and nobody is going to care for your future more than yourself.

If you are currently in high school and under the age of eighteen, legally you are still a child. But I have a few tasks for you, as well. Continue to research different fields of study or possible careers that that interest you that don't require a traditional four-year degree. While doing your research, aim to conclude your high school career with an above-average GPA. This can help you land scholarships that could pay for your college tuition.

Also, take the ACT, SAT, or whatever test is required for admittance to a college within your state. Try your best to score as high as possible so that you can receive scholarships. Retake those test multiple times so that your highest score can be used. This is not only important for scholarship opportunities but also to skip remedial classes during college. I scored low on the math portion of my ACT, thus leading me to take a mandatory intermediate algebra class prior to college algebra. That class didn't reward any college credits and was a complete waste of time and money. Had I taken my ACT more seriously, I probably would have gone straight to college algebra and would have received a scholarship.

Some states even allow you to replace your low scores with the highest score on a portion of the test. For example, if you scored 18 on the math but later scored 24, you can replace that lower score.

Furthermore, another task I have for those that are still in high school is to have a part-time job, start a side business, or enroll in dual-credit college courses. Of course, with your parents' permission, try to start building your work experience and complete a few college courses as early as possible. This will strengthen your skills in sales, marketing, customer service, time management, and many more areas that are basic requirements to getting hired or starting your own business.

I'm not a millionaire by a long shot yet, but as I have studied other successful people, most, if not all of them, had some sort of job or business when they were a kid. My jobs included working at my dad's restaurant, mowing lawns, washing cars, selling cookies, and even repairing homes. This helped tremendously in preparing me for the workforce and landing several good paying jobs at my age.

So, from those tasks I mentioned above, you should be plenty busy during high school and shouldn't be doing time-wasting activities and find yourself with idle time. Nothing wrong with some fun, but have a little self-responsibility to handle your business. At the young age of sixteen, Napoleon Bonaparte graduated from École Militaire and became a second lieutenant in the French Army. I'm sure a few side hustles and extra classes won't hurt your brain and body.

To recap for those in high school:

- Maintain or increase GPA to above average.

- Take ACT, SAT, or state tests numerous times until a satisfactory score is reached.

- Create a side business, apply for a part-time job, or take dual-credit college courses to get a head start.

- Apply for hundreds of scholarships to pay for your college tuition. Sites such as MyScholly.com are great places to start.

- Research your field of study's job growth, salary potential, and cost of education.

Those Over the Age of 18

Moving forward, for those that are over the age of eighteen and thinking about going to college or going back to college, I have a few recommendations for you. Before the semester begins, try to land a job that has a tuition reimbursement benefit. This means your employer will reimburse you for a certain amount of (or all of) your college tuition upon successful completion of those courses. If you can't land a job that pays for your tuition, continue to pursue jobs that will pay enough so that you can cash-flow your college tuition each year. My tuition for example was approximately $6,000/year, which will only require you to find a job making at least that amount annually to cover your costs.

If you are unable to find a job, get a scholarship, or receive any assistance to pay for college, I don't recommend taking out student loans. Avoid student loans like the plague, which is what they can feel like later in life when you're struggling to pay them off. Some may disagree with this advice, but I don't expect everyone to understand, especially people that still have student loans sitting around. If anything, continue to search for employment, build skills from free online learning, and once you land a job or scholarship, then go to college.

Though I don't recommend student loans, there are only two exceptions that I will make. One exception is when the student loan is minuscule, and you can afford to pay it off within a few months. Having a plan to pay it off in such a short time period reduces the chance you will allow it to get out of hand. My final exception is if your employer offers tuition reimbursement and you don't immediately have the funds available at the beginning of the semester. You can take out a student loan temporarily until you receive that reimbursement to ultimately pay it off.

The only reason I recommend these two exceptions is because there is a strategic way to bypass the student loan interest that is accumulated when you borrow for such a short time frame. You can do this by taking out the student loan and paying it off in full before 120 days has passed since you accepted the loan.

The most important piece of advice I can give in this entire chapter is get a college degree in a field of study that will provide you with a job when you graduate. Steer clear of majors such as art, library studies, physical education, photography, etc. If you study a major that does not provide you with tangible skills and that doesn't apply in the current job market, you will very likely find yourself unemployed. Research college majors that are in the medical field, computer science, engineering, finance, etc. The job market is always changing, so that's why it is important to set time aside to research this information yourself—before enrolling in college.

College is not the Be-All-End-All

Another important thing to note is that college is not always the right answer for everyone. You can very well make a high income in careers that don't require a degree. The trades and certification programs are becoming more and more popular as young people realize that more jobs are being automated and replaced by robots. There are many careers to consider, such as becoming a plumber, welder, real-estate agent, insurance agent, police officer, financial advisor, etc. Those few careers alone can easily make over $50,000/year in a city with a growing economy.

Save Money by Choosing an Affordable Location

Once you have a strategy to pay for college, and a field of study that will provide a good paying job, you will now have to choose a college/university to attend. Most students will find that the cheapest colleges are usually close to home or within their state. If you look out of state, you will find astronomical fees just to attend. Do not enroll in another state. Unless the school waives out-of-state fees or offers a full ride scholarship.

If you do opt to attend a school close to home, and your parents offer you a place to stay while you finish your degree, take full advantage of that opportunity. There is not a rush to start "adulting" just yet. When you graduate, then start planning your exit.

To the parents out there, it's OK to charge your new college student a low rent to live with you. Better yet, if you have the financial compacity, save that rent money over the next few years, and when they graduate, offer them the total amount to invest, deposit as a down payment to buy their first home, start their own business, or any other creative gift.

After you have decided upon the college that you will attend and your housing situation, you will need to enroll in your classes either online, on campus, or during the weekend. Assuming you have a job, I advise taking as many online classes as possible, if offered. For those that lack self-discipline to do your work on time, start taking physical classes first and eventually ease your way into online courses. It is important that you use your time very strategically when you are young, without wasting it away in a three-hour class that only requires thirty minutes of your attention. With online learning becoming more popular, you can spend your extra time doing other activities that benefit you in the long run.

Lastly, after you have finished enrolling in all your classes, the only thing left to do is go take care of business. Aim to do your best academically, and at your current job or business. All of this will make you competitive when applying for jobs related to your major.

Older Adult? It's Not Too Late for You...

For older adults, who have been in the workforce some years now and might be looking to further their education, you have several options at your disposal. While following the same principles as I advise young adults, make sure to major in a field of study that will develop your skills if you decide to go to college. It's easy to lean toward the easy college majors like art, but it doesn't make financial sense to go to school for those types of subjects. If you have that much passion for art, go learn about it at the library or online; both are free.

If you have a job that you see is being automated or replaced by robots in the coming years, look into ways to remain relevant at your current employer. Usually, employers offer certifications or other personal development courses to enhance your skills in the industry you are in. If your employer doesn't offer you any resources or personal development curriculums, maybe it's time to move on ahead of the layoff curve that is bound to happen. There are people at places like Blockbuster that may have seen the end coming but stuck around hoping for the best. And we see how well that plan worked out for them.

I don't want you to panic or get nervous; however, I want you to always continue learning and sharpening your skills so that you are adaptable in any environment. I always give people the example of barbers, hair stylists, plumbers, nurses, landscapers, etc., because they will more than likely always be employed.

Overall, self-education is more accessible than ever before. This allows anyone from any age group to start learning a new skill online in the comfort of their own home. So, between college, employer-sponsored certifications, and self-learning, you have plenty of options to secure your future employment opportunities. You're never too old; the world is just getting older.

The Search for Employment

Moving on to the next topic: finding employment. There are millions of jobs out there waiting for acceptable candidates to fill them. With the economy reaching full recovery from the Great Recession that truly began to bite in 2008, we have seen a trend of employee droughts. This means employers are having a tough time filling positions due to low unemployment and a limited amount of people with the skills needed to perform certain job duties. This is where education and employment work hand-in-hand.

In order to align yourself with these numerous opportunities, you have to evaluate three factors in your life. Those three factors are skill set, location, and education.

The first factor, skill set, can be evaluated by determining what are you good at. Do you possess mechanic skills, are you good at sales, can you program a computer? If you don't possess any skills for the jobs you wish to apply for, it can be very difficult to secure the position. You can have all the education in the world, but employers are looking for people who can perform the job tasks outlined on their job posting. Steadily sharpen your skills so that you're always prepared to take advantage of upcoming job postings. Volunteering to work for someone to learn those skills is a surefire way to get your foot in the door.

The second factor is your location. Are you in an area that has job growth and a booming economy? Many times, people find themselves in a location that has very limited opportunities for employment and remain in that location for extended periods of time. You must be willing to relocate to where opportunities are. Who knows, you may enjoy the new area you move to.

You can do online research on different cities to see which one's employers have been seeking applicants with your skills and education. In today's technologically driven environment, I would recommend submitting applications in the areas that spark your interest to see if you get any bites. Many employers can do virtual interviews, online assessments, and offer relocation benefits to applicants willing to move.

If all else fails, start a low-capital business where you live, and try to increase your income that route if you have your mind set on never leaving your current location. The ideal business for this strategy would be online based, which means you can work anywhere in the world as long as there is Wi-Fi.

The last factor is education. We discussed plenty of strategies on how to pursue higher education, and what to study. You must obtain a degree in a topic that is in demand in order to lock in future employment opportunities. The more advanced the degree, the more opportunities that will await you when you finish. Think about software engineers; they are in demand in almost every city, but the degree can be very difficult to obtain. Nursing is another difficult degree that offers plentiful opportunities. I cannot stress the importance of getting a degree in STEM, medicine, finance, or other fields that are in increasing market demand. Further, as the American population continues to age, these fields are set to explode in terms of the number of jobs.

Moreover, be sure to have a solid résumé prepared at all times, and dress appropriately for all interviews. That should go without saying, but you'd be surprised at how some people show up to interviews. So, for men, have on a neutral-colored dress shirt with some black or khaki dress pants. For the ladies, try to stick to neutral colors as well, and don't show up as if you are going to a party. A nice suit won't be a bad idea.

I'm a Southerner. I was raised to be polite, to address people by Mister or Miss and open/hold doors for people. No matter where you were born or grew up, having good etiquette, showing respect, and displaying confidence while being humble can go a long way.

In conclusion to this chapter, I want to leave you with this: When you are young, do not try to go the safe route or waste your youthful years. Handle your business while also taking a few risks. If you want to travel to a new country, do it. If you want to write a book like I have done, do it. If you want to become an actor/actress, do it. Heck, joining the military is a great option as a young man or women.

A person in their 30s 40s, 50s, and older would trade places with you 99 percent of the time because there is one thing you have that they lack: time. You have so much time that you can make numerous mistakes and still recover to get your life back on track. Someone who is forty and has four kids can't relocate to a new city overnight like you can. A person who is fifty can't eat fast food and ramen noodles every day like you may do. This not to disrespect or talk down our older counterparts, but do take note of the advantage you have right now.

To those who are not young adults, it's never too late to turn your life around, either. Buying this book and deciding to get your financial future on track will be one your greatest accomplishment ever. The best part is you live in a country where it's never too late to change. You can go out and pick up an extra job, start investing, start a business, and do many other things without any restriction whatsoever.

As you proceed through these steps of financial longevity, you will realize that if you can increase your income, you will be able save more, get out of debt quicker, and build a larger amount of wealth. So continuous education and seeking better employment opportunities that have high pay can greatly help you achieve your long-term goals financially.

Finally, to all of you that finish this text and implement these financial habits in your life, you will have great success. I know it's sometimes hard to have vision when you are in a dark place in your life. I was once there, too. But I'm here to tell you, you will succeed, and you will overcome any and all obstacles that may lie ahead for you. You have already won the battle by opening your mind to new concepts; now all that is left is to win the war after executing these strategies.

Chapter 7: Retirement Planning

Upon completion of the previous steps, you will have a fully funded emergency fund, little to no debt, and if you opted to additionally prepare for physical emergencies, you will have a fully prepped "bugout bag" and disaster preparedness items.

In this chapter, we will cover the basics of retirement planning and investing. Your biggest asset during retirement planning is time, which translates into compounded interest. Albert Einstein once said, "Compound interest is the eighth wonder of the world. He who understands it, earns it. He who doesn't, pays it."

I have studied every professional investor, financial adviser, financial mentor, finance professor that I could possibly research. Believe it or not, every single one of them has a different approach to investing but the exact same mindset. Consistency, delayed gratification, diversification, and one phrase: "No one can predict the market."

Investing is so easy, a monkey can do it, literally. A Princeton College professor, Burton Malkiel, wrote a best-selling book called *A Random Walk Down Wall Street.*

Inside, he stated, "A blindfolded monkey throwing darts at a newspaper's financial pages could select a portfolio that would do just as well as one carefully selected by experts." As years went by, the monkey's random selection of stocks has outperformed expensive professional investment funds operated by some of the top experts in investing. Now, don't go outside throwing darts at a piece of paper to pick stocks, but do keep in mind that the market is fickle and unpredictable.

Investing is far from intimidating, and the average person has the ability to compile a healthy performing portfolio as long as you start. It's not solely about what you pick but more of when, what, and why you picked that stock or fund. The stock market goes through cycles of economic downturns and economic progressions. Curtis "Wallstreet" Carrol explained it best: "Markets tend to move 70 to 80 percent off of sentiment rather than factual information." Depicted, the market looks like small hills, big mountains, peaks, valleys, and ditches. Which can feel like a bumpy roller coaster ride. And what do we know about safety in regard to roller coasters? Remain seated at all times until the ride has come to a complete stop.

If you are able to stick with it, stay on the roller coaster, and use a strategy known as dollar-cost averaging (DCA). You will be OK for the long term. However, if you pull your money in and out attempting to "time" the market, you will more than likely lose every time. Dollar-cost averaging simply means buying an investment consistently, on a regular schedule, no matter the price or performance. For example, if I buy a share of Apple at the price of $100, but the market drops and the share drops to $80, I will continue to buy even when it's at $80. If the price of Apple goes up to $120, I will continue buy even though it is $120. This a very basic strategy to start off investing for beginners, but as you learn about the market you will learn more effective strategies. You don't want to continue randomly picking stocks and buying at any prices forever, but the idea is to just start.

I don't want to intimidate you like most financial experts by using broad terminology that only we understand. This will only scare you away from making your first stock purchase. As time goes on, you will gain understanding of how to "buy low," reading a company's income statements/balance sheets, understanding the P/E ratio (price to earnings), buying high-quality dividend-paying stocks, covered calls, etc. When your portfolio reaches over $100,000, you have to definitely make sure you are investing in high-quality positions and worry about the fees you are paying. Randomly picking won't cut it at this point.

Speaking of buying low and selling high, a downward trend in certain stocks/bonds is a known as a bear market. An upward trend in certain stocks/bonds is known as a bull market. This is why you hear investors stating they are "bullish" on a certain stock or "bearish." Consequently, when investors feel bullish on certain stock positions, they usually invest more into that stock, hoping that it will rise in value. This can be problematic if you are bullish or bearish on the wrong investments, causing increased losses in your portfolio.

Let's say you had a time machine and could predict how the market would react on future dates. An ideal move to make is to sell when stocks/bonds are high and buy when they are low. This will create a profit for you every year since you know for a fact when to pull in and out of positions. This is the only way to predict the market, and if someone guarantees you that they can predict upward moves in certain stocks, they are lying.

The only way to remedy and mediate your profits and losses is to research the companies and funds you invest in. If you assess that the company is unprofitable, lacks innovation, and has a lot of debt but the stock value is overpriced, maybe it's time to sell that particular stock. Look back at the dot-com bubble on how people were investing in companies that weren't profitable, but their stock values were up hundreds of points. They held on to those stocks. More people bought in to follow the crowd, everyone became greedy even when it was obviously a bubble, and all of them got slaughtered when the bubble burst in 2002.

If you continue to feel uncomfortable with making investment decisions alone, there are plenty of investment professionals and certified financial planners that can assist. You can google for someone local with excellent ratings and who possesses a proven track record of great results. Family friends don't seem to work out for most people.

However, if you are like I was when I first started investing with $20 in my account, I recommend starting with a robo-advisor, or target date fund. The reason I went this route was because I wanted my investments set on autopilot while I waited to accumulate enough cash to invest with an advisor or investment firm. Since that time of buying that first investment, I learned tremendous amounts of information, and I can now trust my own judgement when making personal investment decisions. This may be the case for you as well as you gain understanding of the market.

As your account gains value and surpasses $25,000, $50,000, or $100,000, and you continue to be uncomfortable managing your own portfolio, I suggest getting a professional, highly rated financial adviser to take over from there. We don't want to accumulate a large amount only to lose it all. Now, if you are like me and you study finance day in and day out, you can probably handle managing your own portfolio the entire way. But if the day comes where I lack the time to manage my own investments, I definitely will let another financial adviser take over.

Brief Overview of My Investment Mix

For those who may be wondering, I'm currently a financial coach as I write this text and cannot give investment advice or make investment decisions for you. I can only tell you what I would do if I were in your situation and provide guidance and information to understand how the stock market operates. In event that I do become certified as a financial planner, you will definitely be able to find out by visiting my website www.DanTheMentor.com.

Additionally, my investment choices could be vastly different from the investments that you personally need to make. But I want to share what I invest in as of now, for transparency. My investment portfolio in this year of 2018 is massively risky and contains mostly US stocks, international stocks, REITs (Real Estate Investment Trusts), and very few bonds. Though I hold some positions in individual stocks, I additionally make investments in ETFs (Exchange-Traded Funds). I also invest in commodities such as precious metals, oil stocks, and crypto currency. I will say that I'm increasing my balance in money market accounts to reduce the overall volatility in my portfolio since it is relatively high risk. This investment mix isn't optimized for someone in their fifties, for example, who is close to retirement. That's why it's important to develop a basic understanding of investing and create a plan that matches your risk tolerance and long-term goal. I'm only sharing for transparency, and it is not my recommendation to invest the exact way that I do because everyone's financial picture is different and by the time this book is published, my positions could change. I cannot repeat enough; no one knows how the stock market is going to react, and if someone tells you that they do, they're lying.

Have a Plan

Before jumping in to buying stocks, bonds, and other investments, it is important to have a plan. The plan will keep you on track to hit your goal and provide a smooth transition into retirement living. A quick and easy way to calculate how much savings you need in retirement is the 25x equation. Simply multiply your current income or desired in income by 25, and this will equate to how much total you need to have saved by retirement. If your retirement savings should be $1 million, then assuming a 4 percent withdrawal rate, you should be able to withdraw $40,000 a year. This can be done for twenty-five years until you have completely exhausted your $1 million savings. If the money is invested, it could potentially last you longer.

This is just a basic way to calculate your retirement goal to get a rough estimate on how much you will need. Remember, there are other factors including health care, disability, housing, inflation, travel expenses, etc. Keep those factors in mind when calculating. You don't have to be exact on the amount you will need, but we are just starting a conversation and estimating what will retirement look like for you and your family financially.

Some years, you may spend $20,000; others you may spend $60,000, which will even out over time to your total amount. Remember, historic returns do not guarantee future returns. This is why we eliminated debt, built an emergency fund, and created a plan—so that during economic downturns, you don't panic and withdraw your principal from your retirement funds.

As far as where to retire, the world is your oyster. If I knew the perfect place to retire, I would be there right now to get a head start. However, I have a few possible locations in mind after researching what states/countries offer the lowest cost of living, access to affordable retirement homes, national parks, recreation activities, low crime, stable economy, etc. Those states are Arizona, Colorado,

Idaho, South Dakota, North Carolina, Washington, Florida, Georgia, Tennessee, Alabama, Oklahoma, Texas, Nevada, Utah, and Mississippi.

Mississippi is my birthplace for those that may scratch their heads wondering what's in Mississippi. Mississippi is also the number one state where your retirement funds last the longest. According to a study conducted by GoBankingRates.com, "One million dollars will run out in less than a dozen years in Hawaii but will last more than twenty-six years in Mississippi. This is calculated based on the average cost of living in both states."

A few countries I'm considering are Dominican Republic, Thailand, the Philippines, Argentina, Brazil, Puerto Rico, Switzerland, and some other countries in Africa. I picked these countries for the same reason as the states above: low cost of living and where my US dollars will last longer. The chances of me actually staying in those countries are slim because I love America, but I like to keep an open mind, so nothing is concrete yet. Largely, just do your research and find out what place best fits your needs and makes you happy.

Thinking about retirement, older age, and death could be a very daunting and depressing conversation. On the bright side of this conversation, you are taking action and will be prepared. This will lead to a more comfortable and exciting retirement.

Findings from the Economic Policy Institute Report (2017) state that the average fifty- to fifty-five-year-old has $124,831 in savings, and for ages fifty-six to sixty-one the average is $163,577. These number are not bad but could be better. Can you live off of $163,577 for another twenty-five years? Assuming an annual withdrawal of a minimal $40,000/year after retiring, you will exhaust this balance after only four years, five to six years if you are lucky with a few good investments.

Where to Invest for Retirement

Many of you are probably wondering, there are so many places to invest for retirement, where is the best place to start? In the United States, we have the 401(k), 403(b), IRA, HSA, real estate, annuity, whole life insurance, and the list goes on. My recommendation is to start with your employer's 401(k)/403(b) only if they offer an employer match program. For 2019, the maximum contribution to a 401(k), 403(b), and 457 accounts is $19,000 a year.

For example, my employer offers a dollar-for-dollar match up to $1,200 every year. This means that if I contribute $500 for that year, they will contribute an additional $500 to my account, giving me a total of $1,000. Talk about free money!

If your employer offers the matching program, contribute to the maximum amount they will match and pause. The next account you will want to contribute to is an IRA. The only exception when contributing more than the employer match is if they have very low investment fees and a wide variety of investment options. In my case, my employer's 401(k) plan has 0 to .05 percent investment fees and offers really good investment options that I am interested in. Therefore, I contribute over the amount of the employer match because it's cheaper than any of my other investment accounts, which have fees ranging from .25 to .65 percent.

If your employer has limited investment options and high fees, only contribute up to the match. You can find better options within your IRA and other investment accounts.

Also, my employer offers a ROTH 401(k) option, which is very beneficial to young investors since your income tax bracket is at its lowest. Roth simply means you pay taxes on the money you invest now at your current tax rate, and later when you retire, withdraw the principal and gains tax free. It's important to sit down with an accountant if you have a hard time determining if you should invest in Roth or pre-tax retirement accounts. Many people believe that income taxes will increase in the future, thus they use the Roth option. Meanwhile, others believe it's best to defer taxes now, which is the pre-tax 401(k) option, while the option exists and pay the taxes you will owe later.

There isn't necessarily a right or wrong answer; it's more of a preference. The fact that you started investing for retirement makes me happy, so you are good in my book. No pun intended.

After meeting your employer match with your 401(k), your next best option is funding your IRA or Roth IRA. Similar to the 401(k), the pre-tax IRA and Roth have the same benefits. In the pre-tax IRA, you can defer taxes now and pay the taxes later when you withdraw during retirement. Or you can opt for the Roth IRA and pay taxes now at your current tax rate in order to withdraw all of your funds tax free during retirement.

As I write this book in the year of 2018, the maximum amount you can contribute to an IRA is $5,500, and if you are over the age of fifty, it is $6,500. In 2019, those maximum amounts increase to $6,000 and $7,000. IRAs are very attractive retirement accounts due to the flexibility and wide range of options to choose from. You are 100 percent in control of your investments and can find brokerages that charge lower fees compared to your 401(k).

This is a plus because in your employer's 401(k) you are boxed in to the investments they offer, which may not perform as great as *your* investment choices. There are even strategies to fund your IRA with real estate investments. I'm not recommending investing your IRA in real estate but just setting out an example of the endless amount of options you have when opening an IRA account.

The IRA account also has a benefit that many people overlook: your ability to invest any time/day the market is open. Meaning if certain stocks plummet on a particular day during the week, you can invest in your IRA that day without missing out on the potential upside performance. To simplify, what I'm trying to explain is this: Your 401(k) limits you to only invest on your payday, every other week or month, while your IRA allows you to invest more strategically, and buy stocks/bonds when they are on sale.

Obviously, I don't want you to jump at every market dip and try to day-trade within your IRA account. However, I do want you to consider increasing the frequency of deposits into your IRA to take advantage of the days/weeks when the market is down. For example, instead of automatically depositing funds in your IRA when you get paid, create an automatic deposit that occurs on a weekly basis or every other day to properly use the dollar-cost averaging method. As you move forward in this chapter, you will develop a better understanding of why we buy stocks/bonds when they are "on sale."

How Much Should You Invest?

Depending on your income, you may be able max out your IRA every year. I do recommend what most financial experts advise, which is aiming to save a minimum of 15 percent of your income toward retirement across all of your accounts. However, I am also a huge fan of F.I.R.E, which stands for Financially Free Retiring Early.

Since discovering F.I.R.E, I have made it a top priority in my life to become a minimalist, to live off of less than 60 percent of my income, and maximize my savings vehicles to allow me to retire early. I don't plan to just retire and not produce any income, but rather to work a job I truly love and use the income from my passive investments to offset what I need for living expenses.

You don't have to become a minimalist, or take extreme measures to retire early, but I mention this to motivate you to save more than 15 percent of your income. This route will offer you numerous options down the road when deciding on if/when you want to retire. Every percentage point more you save each year shaves off months and sometimes years of savings, allowing you to reach your retirement goals faster.

If you manage to save 50 percent of your income each year for five years, this means you have successfully saved roughly five years of your retirement income. This is by no means a perfect formula but gives you an idea on how you are progressing as far as your savings goals.

Moving back to the IRA account, it also provides tremendous flexibility when you need to borrow money. As long as you only borrow the principal, you won't have to pay the penalty tax on your IRA account. So, speak with your accountant for options regarding this strategy.

What if you can't Invest 15% or More?
If you are unable to contribute 15 percent or more to your retirement accounts due to an already tight budget, I have a strategy that may help.

All of us have vastly different amounts of income, but as a whole our income tends to go upward as we get older and gain more job experience. If the amount of 15 percent sounds daunting, I ask you to start with contributing at least 5 percent of your income. This means you have 95 percent left to spend on other necessities. While you may start at 5 percent, you won't stop at this amount. Every three to six months, I want you to gradually increase that contribution percentage up by 1 percent or more. For example, if you start at 5 percent in January, in March you will increase your contribution to 6 percent, then in June your contribution will increase to 7 percent, and so on. You can determine how fast or slow you want your increases to go, but the overall goal is to have an upward trajectory.

Never Borrow from Your Future

I never recommend borrowing from any retirement accounts; rather, I always advise people to pretend the money is gone once you contribute to your retirement accounts. This makes it less tempting to withdraw the funds as your balance grows or when you have an "emergency" that demands the use of your retirement savings.

When investing in your retirement accounts, it important to not only deposit the money you invest, but to reallocate your positions quarterly or annually. Maybe you are nearing retirement and want to take on less risk, so you invest more in bonds than stocks. Maybe you are young and prefer more risk, so you buy more stocks and fewer bonds. As you age, the idea is to take on less and less risk so that you actually keep what you have accumulated over the years.

Many people were in high-risk investments during the most recent recession, which caused them to lose over 50 percent of their earnings. Others who had a more diverse and less risky portfolio incurred losses as well, but not as much. Those who believe they predicted the recession bet against the market, or "shorted" the housing market, and received massive gains. I am not recommending you try to predict the market, but I do recommend you stay informed and adjust your positions to fit your long-term plans.

One of my favorite life coaches, Tony Robbins, spoke with renowned investor Ray Dalio to see what his investing strategies were. Ray Dalio is the founder of one of the world's largest hedge funds, Bridgewater Investments. His total net worth is around $18 billion. Tony Robbins is an entrepreneur, philanthropist, and life coach with an approximate net worth of approximately $480 million as of 2018. Ray sounds like a smart guy, so I thought I would share some of his wisdom in regard to investing.

Ray created an investment strategy called the All-Weather Portfolio or All-Seasons strategy. This portfolio was sort of a one and done approach that provides the "perfect" balance of investment during all times of the year and into the future. I quote the word *perfect* because nobody is perfect at predicting the stock market, but you get the idea.

The investment allocation he recommended was 30 percent US stocks, 40 percent long-term US treasury bonds, 15 percent intermediate-term US treasury bonds, 7.5 percent gold, and 7.5 percent in a broad commodity basket. The mix collectively can be seen as a 60/40 mix between stocks and bonds.

Dave Ramsey, who is another person I consider to be an investment expert, suggests a different allocation. He recommends his followers to invest in four types of funds: growth, growth and income, aggressive growth, and international. He touts his generous 12 percent return on his investments as proof that this strategy works. Dave also recommends mutual funds, even though many people are using ETFs, which can be significantly cheaper.

To top it off, Dave invests in real estate, is a best-selling author, and operates a very successful business, Ramsey Solutions. A commonality you will see with people that are multimillionaires and billionaires like Dave and Ray is that they are business owners. So, even though we are discussing retirement strategies, down the road we will explore ways to make additional investments outside of retirement.

There are solutions for people that may not have time or lack knowledge on how to reallocate their positions. Some of those are mutual funds, ETFs (Exchange-Traded Funds), and robo-advisers. Mutual funds are similar to ETFs in what they offer, which is a diversified investment spread across a specific industry. One key distinction between the two is that mutual funds usually are actively managed by a professional fund manager, which translates to higher investment fees.

ETFs have grown in popularity due to very low fees and a wide variety of options for industries you're interested in investing in. Robo-advisers typically use ETFs due to the low fee and invest in different ETFs based on your risk tolerance. A robo-adviser is 100 percent foolproof as they automatically adjust and invest for you over time. The only action you have to take is deposit your money. Now, they don't guarantee higher returns or have some sort of edge against other brokerages; rather, they are foolproof, as in they make it super easy to invest with very little capital and very little knowledge. The most beneficial reason people use robo-advisers is to save time. I have found them helpful for me in regard to reducing panic when markets don't perform well so that I don't move around my positions; they take care of that for me automatically.

There have been discussions on whether ETFs and robo-advisers are for everyone and how they perform during economic downturns. I like them for new investors due to the simplicity and low fee, but as time goes on it's OK to step out into individual stocks and mutual funds.

Target date funds have also gained popularity among 401(k) and IRA accounts for the same reasons robo-advisers have. The ease of investing and low fees makes these great options for everyone new to investing. I personally invest partially in a target date portfolio for my age group, but I also buy in to other outside investments. Everyone's strategy is different, and you should always invest based on what your individual goals are for you and your family.

How to Trade and Sell an Individual Stock

Now that you have a foundational understanding of how to invest for retirement, you are probably itching to know how to buy your first share of stock? To buy a share of stock, the process is fairly simple. Our IRA and 401k accounts are pretty straightforward and usually have different funds to select from, but maybe you just want to take on slightly more risk and buy single stock shares such as Apple or Google.

First, sign up for a taxable brokerage account. It could be one with TD Ameritrade, Robinhood, Ally Invest, etc. You simply visit one of these websites, click accounts, and select open taxable brokerage account.

Next, you will be asked to fund the account. Add a reasonable amount that is enough for you to be able to buy a few shares of the stock you have in mind. If your current bank is online, they may be able to transfer the funds immediately, otherwise, you may have to wait a couple days for the funds to transfer.

Moving on, once the funds successfully transfer, you will receive a notification that says your funds are available for trading. This means you can now buy a share of stock up to the amount that is available in your account. The New York Stock Exchange is only open throughout the week, Monday through Friday, 8:30 a.m. to 3:00 p.m. Eastern Time. It is closed on Saturday, Sunday, and nationally recognized holidays. These dates and times are important because you cannot purchase stocks after hours or days that the market is closed. When you place an order after hours, it will only execute the order the next time/day the market is open.

Now that your funds are available for trading, you are ready to buy some stocks! On the main menu of the brokerage account you are using, you will click a tab that says *trade*. The next screen should list out a few popular/common stocks, and it should allow you to use the search function. In the search field, you will type in the name of the company in which you wish to invest or its ticker symbol (A ticker symbol is simply a company's abbreviated stock ID. For example, Apple is AAPL).

When you find the stock you are searching for, it will have all types of graphs, data, news articles, and other information on that particular company. Every piece of data serves a purpose and is useful when doing your research before buying a stock. We will not get into the weeds of how to properly research the stock, but for now we are just focusing on buying your first share.

Depending on the brokerage website you are using, you will see the option to buy, sell, or trade options. Buy means you want to purchase this particular stock. Sell means you want to sell the shares of the stock you already own. Trade options means you want to do option trading. Option trading can be complex, and you should only select that choice when you have studied how option trading works. Again, we will focus on just buying your first stock in this book.

You will click buy, and it will give you two options. A limit order or market order. A limit order allows you to buy a stock when it drops to a certain price point when the market is open; it is *limiting* your order to a certain amount. A market order is simply a request to buy the stock at its current market price. Depending on the time and day you place your market order, the price of the stock could change and will be purchased for either price. That is why a limit order can be beneficial because it prevents this from happening in case the price of the stock suddenly goes up.

Now, choose which type of order you would like. If it was limit, you will be prompted to enter the amount you wish to *limit* the order, if it was market it will automatically input the current asking price of the share. It will then ask, how many shares you wish to purchase? You can purchase any number of shares you want up to the amount of available funds in your account. Typically, you can only purchase whole number shares at most brokerage firms, but with some stock trading platforms, they allow you to purchase fractional shares (Fractional shares are even smaller pieces of a stock. For example, a fractional share will appear as 5.789 shares of company XYZ, while a whole number share is just 5 shares of company ABC). For simplicity, just enter a whole number such as 1 or 2.

It will then prompt you to enter the time the order should expire. This is on some platforms, so don't worry if yours does not give you this option. I usually enter by end of trading day which is 3:00 p.m. EST. Basically, if they are not able to execute the order by 3:00 p.m. EST. It will automatically expire at that time and you will have to create a new order.

Assuming there aren't any other fields for you to fill out, you can now select *submit order*. Depending on the firm, they will charge you a commission or trading fee for each order you place. This can range from $0 to $10. Robinhood, which has become very popular over the years, has disrupted the investing industry with their $0 trading fee. That means, if you purchase a share of ABC company for $10, that is all you will have to pay when they execute your order. If you are using a more traditional brokerage, they usually charge around $5 per trade which means you will be paying a total of $15 for that same single share of ABC company. The way to get the most bang for your buck at traditional firms is to place larger orders or meet their requirements to qualify for a certain amount of free trades. These requirements could be anything; from holding $25,000 in one of their savings accounts or being a customer with multiple types of accounts with them.

Each institution has their respective pros and cons which is why you cannot only base your decision to do business with them off of the trading fee. Though the fees are a big consideration, sometimes you are paying a higher fee for better customer service, innovative technology, and more access to research and data on each particular company. Sometimes it's nice to be able to pick up the phone and speak with another human being to help you with an order of stock.

Congratulations! You have just purchased your first stock! Just like your retirement, building wealth in stocks takes time. You will not always make the best choice and you may lose more than what you purchased it for. The idea is to learn, execute and be consistent. Over time, stocks grow in value and can be very rewarding to those that are patient. If single stocks are too volatile for you, try making your first stock purchase in index funds or ETFs (Exchange-Traded Funds) such as the S&P 500 or Vanguard Total Stock market fund. These provide stake in a broad mix of companies that reduce the volatility in your portfolio. No one knows how the market will react in the future, so do your research and only invest in companies or funds that make sense and have potential for long-term growth!

The Power of the Health Savings Account

Another attractive retirement savings vehicle is an HSA (Health Savings Account). Most people qualify for this account if they are enrolled in a high-deductible health insurance plan. This account allows you to contribute your pre-tax income, invest it, and withdraw the principal and gains tax free. It's essentially a triple tax break. Now, the only catch is that withdrawals from this account can only be used toward qualified health expenses such as doctor visits, dental work, surgeries, etc.

The reason I included this as part of your retirement plan is because once you reach the age of sixty-five, you can withdraw the funds and use them toward any purchases outside of healthcare. It's almost better than an IRA, but that's an additional five-and-a-half-year wait to withdraw the funds in retirement. As stated above, the HSA is referred to as a triple tax break vehicle due to your ability to contribute on a before tax basis, invest without capital gains tax, and withdraw it tax free.

You have more retirement options, as well, such as an annuity or real estate, but the ones I mentioned above are the most common and easiest to start investing in today.

More Ways to Save for Retirement

Some people prefer the old-fashioned way of saving in a high-yield savings account or government bonds due to low risk, but that can be problematic if you are receiving 1 to 3 percent over the course of thirty years. It's a good strategy, but only for a small percentage of your overall retirement portfolio. Once you have an amount that you are comfortable with in cash investments, you can look into other less volatile investments that may not be as risky as stocks.

One of my mentors, Aaron Clarey, who owns Assholeconsulting.com (yes, that really is the name of his company, LOL), discusses an additional retirement strategy in his books where he recommends the minimalist approach that many people are starting to adopt. In a nutshell, the minimalist pathway to retirement is downsizing your lifestyle to a point where it doesn't take as much money to fund your daily living standards. Aaron speaks of the most important reason for living is being able to interact with other humans and enjoying experiences, not a new car purchase or big, fancy house.

He also stocks up on nonperishable goods. If you think about retirement, what are you saving for? To have enough funds to buy the services and goods you will need. By stocking up on certain products before retirement, you are avoiding inflation and increased pricing of those goods. When I heard him mention this, it made so much sense. So, if you want to designate a few dollars to purchase nonperishable items before retirement, that's a good strategy to start with if you are very close to your last date of employment.

Finally, when you decide on which accounts to invest in and how you want to invest, set your payments on automatic deposit to stay consistent. You can use the 15 percent contribution as a baseline, but attempt to increase your contributions over time. For every extra amount you contribute, the less amount of time it will take to reach your retirement fund goals. If you are fortunate enough to have a large income, your goal should be to max out all of your retirement accounts due to the tax benefits and long-term gains.

Should you become nervous at any point during your first steps toward investing, remember: You may lose 20, 50, 90 percent of your account's value when investing in the stock market; however, you lose 100 percent every time you make a consumer goods purchase. Therefore, investing is rarely a bad choice given the other uses that a majority of people spends their money on.

At the end of the day, if you started with $100, and your account dropped to $10, at least you have something to show for it. Plus, as mentioned earlier, the stock market goes in cycles. There will be times of downturns and times of tremendous gains. The key is to stick through the storms.

Retirement planning can get frustrating, especially when thinking of yourself at such an older age, but it is one hundred times more rewarding. You won't have to worry about social security, you won't have to seek employment, and you will be well prepared for a comfortable retirement to enjoy family and vacations.

Stay Healthy

Lastly, an important thing to consider adding as part of your retirement plan is investing in your health. That doesn't mean buy health insurance and not use it. Start using your health insurance if you haven't done so already for your free annual checkups. You must also continue to maintain a healthy diet, exercise, and reduce stress.

Many financial planners discuss everything about making monetary investments, but completely forget that you have to live a healthy lifestyle to reach you retirement age and enjoy your wealth. So, I will briefly cover a few things to consider when implementing a retirement plan that not only guarantees a financial cushion but a healthy solution for those that aren't preparing their body for the future. I'm not a doctor, but I do have common sense. Make sure to seek help and advice from a medical professional if you have any personal health concerns.

First, as stated earlier, get your annual checkups so that you are always up to date on your overall health. Checkups are usually when doctors discover any potential diseases, illnesses, or negative patterns in your health. They also are good at reassuring you that nothing is wrong. It's easy to go to WebMD or Google to diagnose your symptoms, but usually they go straight to the absolute worst case and can scare you quite easily. Just visit your doctor, let them determine if there is something wrong, and follow their instructions.

The importance of getting a checkup is that you can catch any problems or complications early before it's too late to reverse any damage. As an African-American, I notice many of us forgo doctor visits out of fear. This potentially causes more damage to our health by prolonging an illness we may have. Praying the problem goes away is great, but the Bible also states, "Faith without works is dead."

Next, practice adding an exercise to your daily routine. I usually end my day by doing a mile run, some heavy lifting, and stretching just to maintain my weight and build muscle. I started this routine because in my family, cancer and high blood pressure have affected some members, and my grandmother passed away due to cancer. She was just under seventy years old. This was my wakeup call and motivated me to implement a daily workout routine that could reduce my chances of developing any genetically inherited illnesses.

You can accumulate $1 million to start using in retirement at age sixty-five, but if you pass away at sixty-seven, saving that $1 million was somewhat all for nothing. If you don't know where to start on how to exercise properly, hire a personal trainer to assist. This is where the real investing can happen. Paying someone to guide and motivate you to perform daily exercise activities that will reduce your chance of illness and increase your life span is a great investment choice.

Furthermore, implementing a healthy diet will contribute positively to a long, healthy life. Some countries like Japan have seen increases in their overall life span mainly due to maintaining a good diet. Even their portions of food are smaller than most American dishes that are high in fat, sugar, sodium, and other unhealthy ingredients. The US and other countries have definitely taken note, and we are starting to see a widespread push from the masses toward healthy meal choices at popular restaurants.

More people are trying to eat less red meat and more fish from cleaner sources. Although some scientists—some of the top minds in the field—will tell you that nearly every fish sold in stores has some degree of either mercury poisoning or some other nasty pollutant because of the sad state of the earth's seas right now. Do your research on the foods you choose to eat.

People are turning down processed foods and canned goods due to their high sodium levels. People are turning away from fast food that is mainly fat and salt. People definitely want to live a longer life, and it all starts with what you eat. As our parents told us when we were kids, "You are what you eat."

Finally, reducing stress in your life benefits you down the road greatly. Stress has been proven to cause depression, high blood pressure, cardiovascular disease, obesity, and many more afflictions. To reduce stress, exercising definitely helps, but I have found that meditating and doing activities that I love also have benefitted in reducing my stress levels. Start to think about what physical activities you can incorporate in your daily life.

Securing your financial future and practicing financial longevity are big steps toward preventing unnecessary stress in your life and positively contribute to an overall healthy lifestyle. Without the constant worry of money, you can avoid plenty of arguments and avoid many of the pitfalls of not having a sufficient amount of money for emergencies. As you can see, finance and health work hand-in-hand whether it's retirement, marriage, emergencies, etc. One cannot be prioritized over the other, and both should be at the forefront of your retirement plan.

Your future is in your hands, and it is up to you to prepare now to secure your retirement.

Chapter 8: Legacy Building and Planting Seeds

W hat is your legacy, and how will the future define you when you are no longer here on earth? Very deep subject, but very important topic. I begin this chapter asking that question because often we forget how short life is. Hippocrates once said, "Art is long, but life is short." What did he mean by that statement?

As you gather your thoughts on what your legacy looks like and how you plan to create a strong foundation for yourself and those after you, I want to discuss several financial strategies that will secure your financial legacy. From buying a home to starting family businesses, there are plenty of strategic ways to build a strong financial legacy.

I admire companies that have been around for decades such as Walt Disney, Walmart, McDonald's, Coca-Cola, State Farm, etc. The founders of these companies will be remembered for even more decades, maybe centuries into the future. They started as small businesses with very little revenue, and doing business wasn't always so smooth in the early days. For example, Walt Disney filed for bankruptcy several times before finally landing his billion-dollar idea, Mickey Mouse. That one cartoon character lives on today, creating billions of dollars of profit each year for the Disney Company.

So, let's follow the examples of these longstanding companies and begin to think about legacy, about what kinds of investments and wealth we can leave behind for those we love.

Now, the most traditional and conservative investment that most people think of is buying a home. This allows you to avoid paying the landlord and acts as a savings account that grows in value over a period of time until you retire—at least, that was until the housing market crashed in 2008/2009. As time goes on and the market continues to "recover," people are starting to buy expensive homes and even using federal programs such as the FHA, VA and USDA mortgage programs for the 0-3% percent minimum down payment.

However, if you follow me on social media, and the principles I outline, you will see that I believe in putting down at least 20 percent. I'm neutral when it comes to paying a smaller down payment such as 5 to 10 percent, but I would stress that you have a fully funded emergency fund, very little debt, if any at all, and the home mortgage cannot exceed more than 20 to 30 percent of your gross income. I'm neutral because I want everyone to be in a position of financial strength at all times, thus the reason I recommend 20 percent or more. Putting anything less increases the chance the house will become a source of stress in tough times.

I highly recommend following the steps in this text and on my website so that you are always making the best decision when taking big steps such as this. I urge you to develop a strong financial foundation before pursuing home ownership.

So, to be clear, if you plan to buy a home, try to put down 10 to 20 percent. Yes, 20 percent or more is the magic number if you are able to tuck away that much. That amount as a down payment will remove PMI (private mortgage insurance). You can also eliminate PMI by paying your lender up front for the cost of it, if applicable. A significant down payment will also create a buffer in the event an economic downturn happens and will protect against significant drops in value. For instance, if you put down 0 percent and the market drops, effectively reducing your home value down 20 percent, you will have to come up with a 20 percent difference in payment to sell the house to someone if you can no longer afford it.

Now, most real estate experts express how much they love debt because of the low interest, and you should try to put down as little as possible, so your cash isn't locked in to the house. Given, this strategy sounds great, but most people aren't dealing with real estate every day and aren't experts in selling real estate. If it was so easy, many people wouldn't have lost their home during economic crashes, job losses, or long-term injuries. Most people who end up in financial hardship who purchased a home usually file bankruptcy because 1) they love debt and 2) they took on too much of it and overdosed.

Unless you have some sort of special advantage or did some type of research in the area and have enough funds to cover the mortgage loan, putting down 0 percent is not a great idea in most situations. In some cases, people get lucky by putting 0 percent down, and the property appreciates, and they are able to sell it for a profit. But those who are unlucky lose everything because they bought a property that they couldn't afford.

An ideal credit score to qualify for a low-interest mortgage is anything above 700 to 720. A score below 700 will more than likely result in a higher interest rate. However, putting down a large down payment (20 percent) and opting for a fifteen-year or shorter mortgage term will help reduce the interest rate if you happen to have a low credit score.

Some lenders recommend a thirty-year mortgage to lower the monthly payment and increase the amount of home you can purchase. I'm against this strategy only because if you have to extend your loan term to afford a large purchase, more than likely you can't afford it. I'm not against a thirty-year mortgage, per se; I'm only against stretching your finances to maximum capacity in order to afford something you truly can't handle.

If you can qualify for a home with a fifteen-year mortgage that will only require 30 percent or less of your income, it's OK to opt for a thirty-year mortgage just to have the extra buffer. The same rule applies to the 30-year mortgage; only finance a home that will not exceed 30 percent of your income. My recommendation: qualify for a fifteen-year mortgage or less while only using 30 percent or less of your income, and use the 30-year mortgage to your advantage. This will provide insurance in case you aren't able to keep up with the larger 15-year payments in the unlikely event you lose your job or your income decreases.

Not only do you have to take into consideration your down payment and credit score, but there are more steps ahead that the lender will have you walk through before approving you for your mortgage. Assuming you have an exceptional credit score of 720, and a down payment for the home, you will be asked about your employment history, debt to income ratio, savings, previous bankruptcies, and many other factors lenders look at before extending you a loan.

Starting with employment history, as a baseline, lenders prefer that you have at least two years of consecutive employment. This can be full-time, part-time, or you could be a business owner. Here is where having a steady career can work toward your advantage versus jumping from job to job or pursing business ownership. It's not impossible to qualify for a mortgage as a business owner, but as we all know, business income can be very volatile, especially in the early stages. An idea that I give to clients is to start your business on the side, and while it's in the growth phase, keep your current job for stability. At least keep your job until you get approved for the mortgage and move into the home.

The difference between business income and W-2 income to lenders is that W-2 income has a greater chance of coming in at the end of each month versus your business income. They can almost guarantee to themselves that you will be able to pay back the mortgage because you have a stable career and income. When you are in business, you have unpredictable expenses, and you do a lot of tax write-offs at the end of the year which reduces your net income. Lending is a game of risk and of making the best selection of who is more or less of a risk when lending out a mortgage loan. Presenting yourself as stable as possible almost guarantees your approval.

Your debt-to-income ratio or DTI is another huge factor. Remember we discussed this in the *Building Credit the Right Way* chapter. Lenders will add up all of your monthly debt obligations and minimum credit card payments and provide you with your DTI. The only caveat is that they will integrate your projected monthly mortgage, taxes, insurance, and PMI payment into the calculation (PMI only applies when you put less than 20% down. Some lenders don't require PMI). For example, if all of your debts and projected mortgage cost add up to $2500/month and your gross income is $5000/month, your DTI is 50%. Anything above 36% DTI is usually negative and will more than likely result in a denial of the mortgage loan. However, there are several exceptions. Depending on the lender, their DTI cap limit could be 50%, which will result in an approval.

So, ask you lender upfront how high their DTI cap limit is before having them pull your credit report. Maybe you decide to purchase a multifamily home, live in it, and rent out the other units. You can use a certain percentage of the projected rental income to add to your personal income to qualify for a higher mortgage. These are both strategies to bypass the DTI limit. As we discussed, we don't want to overleverage ourselves on mortgage debt and should aim to keep our payment under 30% of our income and pay off as much debt as possible. If you are following that principal, you shouldn't have any issue getting qualified for the loan.

Savings may not be a requirement for some lenders, but it is definitely looked at and should be a priority on your list for preparation to buy your home. Typically, three months' worth of reserves to cover the mortgage is an ideal amount. Though I recommend having six to twelve; for the mortgage process, lenders view three months as acceptable. Anything more will just make you a more attractive applicant. The great thing is, your retirement account balances can be used to qualify for your lender's minimum reserves requirement.

I personally have not experienced bankruptcy; however, I do know that it could negatively affect your chances of being approved. Some mortgage loan officers have told me that if you have experienced a bankruptcy in the last seven years, you will more than likely not be approved. Collections, missed payments, and other negative marks on your credit can create additional setbacks when applying for your mortgage. Do your best to pay what you owe on time and settle any debts in the past that are lingering in your life. I'm sure if someone owed you money, you would want to get your money back as well. There is no way around that.

Once you have successfully surpassed all of the prescreening factors, you will make an offer on the home and hopefully close within the next few weeks or so. Be sure to research the area, get an inspection, check the current property taxes, and speak with a knowledgeable real estate agent that has your best interest at heart.

Assuming the inspection passes without any concerns, property taxes check out, and everything is good to go, you will probably want to negotiate closing costs with the seller. If the seller accepts your offer that is less than asking price, sometimes they will ask you to cover closing. If the offer was rejected, and the seller is firm on asking price, you could possibly ask for them to cover closing cost. Everything depends on the market, your agent, and doing your research—meaning there are multiple outcomes. Some of which, you may pay both asking price and closing costs or you may catch a really good deal below asking price with the seller paying the closing costs. He or she who has the most knowledge usually wins in most negotiating situations.

Once everything is confirmed with the seller, your lender may check your credit, bank statements, and other financials before closing date to make sure nothing has changed. That is why it is important to not take out any loans or do anything prematurely before you close on the home. There are instances where people will run up their credit card or take out loans for new furniture and renovations only to find out the loan was later denied because they exceeded their DTI. Some people even go buy a new car before closing so they can park it in the driveway of their new home. Terrible idea guys, just terrible.

Should I Pay Cash for My First Home?

For those who are young and want to make a power move (wise decision), start saving now as much as you can, and pay cash or put down as much as you can on your first home. Chances are, if you are still in your late teens or 20s, you don't know where you want to settle down long term. You can use this time of uncertainty to save your extra money over the coming years to pay for your first home in full.

Heck, if you are an older person in your 30s, 40s, and 50s, I wouldn't count you all out, either. You can get as fired up as the young people and save up the cash to pay for your home in full, as well. Your advantage over the younger crowd is that in your later years, you typically are making the most money you have ever made in your entire life. If you dial back your expenses temporarily for a few years and do what is called super saving, being able to pay for your home in cash is very feasible.

I receive numerous requests asking me, "What is the best way to save for a down payment toward a home purchase?" My suggestion is to start the old-fashioned way. Open a high-yield savings account and automatically stash away a percentage of your income each pay period. Investing your down payment in the stock market is beneficial, but extremely high risk. The only way I would give a pass to investing your down payment is if the length of time before you buy your home is ten years or more. I don't necessarily recommend it, but that is completely up to you. I personally prefer to have the cash for my home purchase in a savings account that I can easily access and has low risk.

Would I stop investing for retirement? Not entirely. I would advise you to continue investing 15 percent of your income while saving for your down payment, especially if you are in your 20s. If you are in your 30s, 40s, 50s, etc., I would suggest contributing up to your employer match, then saving the rest toward your down payment. This should be done temporarily, and once you have reached the down payment amount, immediately revert to contributing 15 percent or more toward retirement.

Remember how we discussed diversification and slowly entering certain investments? A home can be viewed the same way. Your first home purchase will most likely be the largest purchase you will make in your entire life! It can either be the best move or worst move of your life, as well.

Is Homeownership the Best Path to Wealth?

Before buying a home or even discussing the topic of home ownership, I highly advise traveling across the US. You can pick five to ten of your top states/cities and just go visit for a week or longer. Some states and cities are very attractive for homeownership because of lower taxes, homestead laws, low cost of living, and many other benefits. Others may not be great places to own a home due to higher taxes, high cost of living, and very few benefits for homeowners. Depending on your career and other long-term goals, I would even recommend international travel for those seeking to live abroad. People have left the US to live in countries that are very low cost and offer a different experience/culture from living here.

- I follow people such as Oshay Jackson (Negromanosphere.com),

- Will Freeman (RevolutionaryLifestyle.com), and

- Peter Schiff (EuroPac.com), who all reside abroad and left American living all together.

Oshay lives in Poland, Will lives in Thailand, and Peter lives in Puerto Rico. Watching them has definitely planted seeds in the back of my head that may lead me to one day live abroad myself with my family. Great people to follow to get a little insight on how they transitioned and why they chose those countries.

This is not to discourage homeownership, but to promote a mindset of awareness and strategy before making this purchase. Complete the steps prior to this, and you should be set. Those steps consist of getting out of debt, building a fully funded Rainy Day Fund, contributing to your retirement accounts, and having a plan! There is no rush, so turn off social media, and tune out people that are supposedly hitting large millstones and appear to be doing better than you. You move at a pace that is comfortable for you and that will guarantee long-term results instead of short-term moments resulting in a flashy Instagram picture and huge mistakes.

Furthermore, buying a home isn't for everybody. I remember hearing the wisest words from Grant Cardone, who is a multimillionaire and real estate investor. Grant said, "Rent where you live, own what you rent." I didn't understand what he meant when I heard it, but I immediately realized that owning a home isn't always your only option. He rents his homes everywhere he goes, but he owns real estate in many areas that provide him income. Similar to the teachings of Robert Kiyosaki, he also recommends people focus on passive income instead of buying a home to live in and later retire off of the sale. The fact that they are millionaires should mean we should take a deeper look at what they have to say regarding homeownership.

Some people opt for renting instead of home ownership because home ownership simply brings fewer benefits and more responsibilities. Let's say you are renting for $1,000 a month, which includes 24/7 maintenance request, flexible leasing options, landscaping/cleaning of premises included, on-site customer service, and in many cases a few utilities waived. On the other hand, you have the option to buy a home with a mortgage for $1,000 a month, which doesn't include any of those luxuries stated above, and has more responsibilities such as landscaping the yard, repairs, taxes that can easily reach $300-$500 a month (depending on the home's value), insurance, and many other headaches. Which one sounds more attractive?

Additionally, a simple way to think of it is this: Would you borrow $300,000 at an interest rate of 5 percent to invest in the stock market? I would hope that you answered no because as you have probably heard from brokerages, financial advisers, and other stock market experts, "Historic performance does not guarantee future returns."

A mortgage loan can be viewed similarly. Homes seem to have a steady track record of appreciation, but that is not guaranteed because it happened in the past. You are taking on a large amount of debt to invest and a huge responsibility only to hope that the home will appreciate in the future.

A good question to ask yourself to determine if you should pursue homeownership is will you be residing in that home for the next five to ten years or more. To be more conservative, I personally would advise my clients to ask themselves if they plan to reside in that home over the next ten to fifteen years or more. This question can be the tie breaker or ultimatum if you have doubt or a disagreement with your partner/spouse about buying a home. The reason this question is important is because homeownership is not like Walmart, where you buy a product and return it because it's defective or you changed your mind.

Home ownership requires a significant amount of responsibility, along with many fees and expenses during the buying process and after the purchase phase. The fees can range anywhere from 5 to 15 percent of the purchase price, plus the down payment. When you get ready to sell, that's another 5 to 15 percent depending on your listing agent. If you sell after you have resided in the property for only one to four years (depending where you bought your house), you risk losing money or breaking even. The entire purpose of homeownership is to gain equity and allow time for the property to appreciate in value so if you decide to sell, you will have a profit. Its main objective is for you to have a place to stay forever, and not pay rent ever again.

So, be sure the area you purchase in is where you plan to plant yourself and family for a long period of time. Don't let it be a 100 percent emotional spur-of-the-moment transaction.

Determining potential rental income can be a good evaluation strategy to see if when you move out of the property, the revenue from rent can carry most of the mortgage. Not a guaranteed strategy but something to consider if you are unsure if you will reside in the home long term.

How can I Own a Home and Create Passive Income?

As you guys probably have figured out from reading my strategies, I never suggest one extreme over the other. So, I have suggestion for those that want to own real estate but also want it to be a good investment. However, be aware that owning a home itself isn't necessarily an investment because it doesn't offer what makes an asset an investment: income. What if you could own a home and create a passive income stream? House hacking is the name of the strategy I want you to consider.

Basically, you can house hack by purchasing a duplex, triplex, quadplex, etc., live in one of the units, and rent out the remaining ones. This will provide you an extra income stream and pay for your cost-of-living expenses such as property taxes, insurance, maintenance, etc. This is not for everybody but just an idea I wanted to plant in the back of your head. Ultimately, you are a homeowner and business owner all in one.

To calculate your gross return on investment (ROI) from a rental property, simply add the total annual rent and divide by the total price of the property. It should look similar to this: Let's say you buy a four-unit $100,000 investment property with $750/month per unit that has an annual rental revenue of $27,000 (minus expenses) while you live in one of the units. This means your total gross ROI is 27 percent when you divide $100,000 by $27,000. Don't get too excited because this is an example without expenses, maintenance, taxes, vacancies, and other downsides/hidden costs to owning rental properties. Buying rental property requires a much deeper financial analysis, so simply calculating ROI is not sure-fire way to determine if the investment is good or not

Most of you probably are leaning more toward renting now that you see the headaches of homeownership. So, it's all about personal preference. Instead of pushing you into a home, I am more for supporting what best fits your life and your long-term goals. Whether it's renting, home ownership, or house hacking, I support you regardless because buying a home isn't your only option. My advice: conduct thorough research and decide what your long-term plans are.

I will list below a few things to consider and check before pulling the trigger on your home purchase:

- Location, location, location (this includes schools, crime, politics, job growth, local economy, numerous for-sale signs, etc.)
- Have little to no debt.

- Cash reserves of at least three to six months; six to twelve if you plan to buy investment property.

- Achieve a credit score of at least 700 or higher.

- Have a sufficient down payment, preferably 20 percent or more (Minimum required is 0-3.5% if using VA, USDA, or FHA).

- Get homeowner's insurance with a reputable company.

- Get title insurance.

- Check for tax liens on the property, along with the cost of property taxes.

- Check the area for criminals who have been convicted of sexual assault crimes or any other heinous acts. This can make the home hard to sell, especially to a family with young children.

- Research the history of the property and neighborhood for any drug-related incidents/ activity, murder, or other serious crimes.

- Determine if the home is part of a HOA (Homeowners Association) and mandates a monthly fee. HOAs also can prohibit you from renting out your property to other people.

- Get a highly rated real-estate agent if needed.

- Negotiate. Aim to get as much equity as possible in the negotiation, otherwise you risk being upside-down on the property.

- Evaluate potential rental income.

Investing for your Children

After you buy a home or decide to continue renting, it's also a good time to start planning for your children's college expenses, and if you want to start investing for them to have a down payment or just emergency cash set aside. Maybe you don't have a child but plan to have one eventually; you can still start saving for them regardless. For those who don't plan to have children at all, you can completely disregard this step in your journey to financial freedom.

A well-known account to use to allow investing for your child's college expenses is a 529 plan. This allows you to invest now for your child's future college expenses. Your child can pull the money from the account tax free, including the gains as long as the money is used for school expenses. Some popular accounts are the Illinois 529 plan, Louisiana START Saving Program, Michigan Education Savings Program, and many more. Within most 529 plan accounts, you will find common investment options such as ETFs (Exchange-Traded Funds), mutual funds, target-date funds, etc. You can start investing the moment your child is born, or earlier.

The custodial brokerage account (UGMA/UTMA Account) is another great tool for investing for your child. This option allows you to open a taxable brokerage account for your kids who are under the age of eighteen. Depending on the state of residence, when they reach the ages of either eighteen or twenty-one, they will have complete control of the account. What's awesome about this account is it teaches your kids the concept of investing, discipline, and how time plays a huge role.

If you invest as little as $5/day for your child from ages one until age twenty, they could have approximately $100,000 when they enter adulthood (assuming a conservative 7 percent return on investment). The only downside for this account is it will be taxed at your normal tax rate, so visit a tax professional for additional information. This is my favorite out of the investment accounts for children simply because it gives you more control over the money you have invested. You can use it for any purchase in the future.

A very rare account to invest for your child is the IRA. This is an option only if your child has earned income from employment. Usually, teens start working at age sixteen, which is an excellent time to introduce them to an IRA account. Some online articles even mention parents that are business owners, employ their child earlier than age sixteen, and open the IRA account. Imagine planning your retirement at sixteen, and by age forty-six, you will have the same amount of time invested as most people who start investing at thirty-six to retire at sixty-six. This is like putting your child's retirement account on steroids.

There are many options to plan a solid foundational financial future for your children, and starting as early as possible will provide great rewards. Start researching today!

Start a Business
Another great investment for building wealth and planting seeds is to start a business. This business can be absolutely

anything—preferably something you enjoy and have passion for. It can be hard to build a business that you are not passionate about due to the long-term sacrifice it takes to elevate a business to a point where it brings significant profit.

Often, we think that to start a business we have to take out a small business loan, but that is usually not the case. Many people are starting low-capital businesses that don't require a huge lump sum of cash to start. A common one that I started when I was kid was a lawn-mowing business. It required a $100 mower, $5 worth of gasoline, and my energy. I charged $20 a yard, and by then end of the day, I would have anywhere from $40 to $100. This resulted in a profit after only working one or two days.

Maybe you are into working from home. In that case, you can start a web-designing business that will give you that flexibility. All you will need is knowledge of web design and a laptop, and you are ready to go. This also a common low-capital investment.

While going through this financial longevity journey, you will be surprised at how creative you become at increasing your income. In many cases, when people go through the earlier step of creating a Rainy-Day Fund, they end up sticking with some of those side hustles. For example, that side business of counseling may turn into a permanent side business and eventually become your main business. I didn't think that I would start a financial coaching business on the side and help others achieve what I achieved financially.

But the best and most lucrative business ideas either haven't been discovered yet or are enhanced versions of a business that already exist. Think about Blockbuster and Family Video. They were great businesses back in the day; now we have online streaming platforms giving you access to thousands of movies in a matter of seconds. No more driving to the store, picking up a movie, and returning it later on and being charged a late fee when you didn't return it on time. Open an app, select the movie you want, watch, and it will automatically remove itself when the rental term ends. Finding that million-dollar idea won't happen overnight. However, taking out time to figure out an idea that makes everyone's life easier is probably the best place to start.

Lessons Learned

Once you have secured your four walls and checked them off your list to financial freedom, you can start to develop thoughts on other investments that may not have the same tax advantages as your retirement accounts, 529 plan, home, business, etc. The reason I consider these investments your four walls is because at this point you have contributed to your retirement, you have bought your home if applicable, your children are set, and you possess a solid financial foundation. Getting out of debt and securing yourself financially first gives you flexibility and, most importantly, options.

I know what it feels like to not have many options and to be restricted to a location, job, or situation. When you have all that stress and fear, it paralyzes you into inaction. Think about an old friend, classmate, or relative; some have moved on to do better things, and others are in the same position they were in when you last saw them. Many say inequality or unfair life circumstances keep people in a certain position in life. Often, people blame the rich folks, top 1%, Wall Street, parents, or maybe say others who are successful are lucky. The reality, however, is that everything in your life is your fault, and it's up to you to change your circumstances. It can be tough to hear that, but life is all about trial and error.

The reason I choose to help people with their personal finances is because it is one of the top reasons, if not the number one reason, for divorce, depression, stress, and generational poverty. Moreover, personal finance was not taught in school on a level that applied to everyone.

Teachers taught us how to measure the diameter of circle but didn't tell us what a budget was. We learned how the Egyptian pyramids were built but didn't learn how to file our tax returns. Basic, everyday life essentials were completely skipped, and young adults entered the world without a clue on how to effectively manage their finances.

This resulted in an entire generation of indebted servants. Many people are struggling because they were given bad information while growing up. My goal is to help as many of you as possible and give the correct information to allow you to catapult your financial future in the right direction.

Now that you are almost to the finish line, it's OK to ease off the gas a little to enjoy some of your accomplishments. There are only a few things left you can do, but at this point you can say that you are financially free!

Sustaining your Financial Freedom

Moving past this point, I want to focus on ways to ensure your financial longevity. These options aren't mandatory but definitely are great ways to double down on your financial foundation so that you are not easily swayed when different bumps on road through life happen.

As stated earlier, starting a business is a good way to secure your four walls if you run out of retirement investments. Owning your own personal business provides you with options in the event your main job doesn't work out. Maybe your business is your only job, and your job security is ultimately within in your control. It's not like you can fire yourself. So becoming a business owner does have great benefits, and the best of them all: (almost) everything is within your control. Maybe you can't control the market or external forces, but you can control your ability to get up each morning and start working at growing the business.

I have always been the type of person seeking a lean and secure route throughout life. Don't get me wrong, I take on plenty of calculated risks, but I try to avoid unnecessary ones.

To balance out the risks I take, I increase my security by increasing my savings, or maybe making a more conservative investment. For example, think about kids as an investment. It can be extremely risky at times, but you alleviate some of the risk by creating a foundation before deciding to have a child. Having a child post-marriage, starting an emergency fund, having very little debt, living off of one income so that a parent can stay at home, etc., are all methods of decreasing risk when trying to have children and sustaining a positive financial future.

Compare that to someone who had a child out of wedlock, does not have emergency savings, is living paycheck to paycheck, etc. The chance of this person living in poverty is increased. Now, many of you know that I went the nontraditional route and had a child out of wedlock, thus causing me to be a single dad. It was tough, and continues to be tough, but I managed to turn the ship around a little by following these steps that I outlined throughout this text. I relieved myself of debt, started to make investments, and met the love of my life, whom I plan to marry soon. It's possible to achieve financial freedom even if, like me, you didn't make the best the decisions growing up. The ball is in your court.

So, doubling down and seeking extra cushion is the goal moving forward. A way to do that is to continue your investments in retirement, and even maxing them out if possible, but after all the previous steps, look into just opening a taxable brokerage account. We discussed in detail how make your first stock purchase in Chapter 7, *Retirement Planning*. Granted, these accounts do require you to pay capital gains tax and do not offer the tax-deferred benefits as your retirement accounts, but the compounding results after years of investing will far outweigh the contributions and taxes.

Currently, as I write this text, you can find these accounts with online brokerages such as TD Ameritrade, Charles

Schwab, Robinhood, Vanguard, Betterment, etc. I cannot give investment advice on what stocks and bonds to pick, but I will say that an easy way to determine your risk tolerance is by your age. For example, if you are twenty years old, you can pretty much afford extra risk because you have decades of time to make up or correct any losses. If you are sixty years old, and on your way to retirement, maybe you should take a more conservative approach or one with less risk.

If you are new to investing or struggle understanding investing concepts, you can pay certified investment professionals to make investments for you for a higher fee. Another option is managed mutual funds that also charge a higher fee, but the goal is to leave the investment choices with a professional investor so that you don't have to make decisions on what to trade and sell. As stated in the *Retirement Planning* chapter, robo-advisers such as Betterment are becoming a popular option that offers both a lower fee and an account that automatically invests for you depending on your age and other algorithms.

Opening this additional investment account can also be used to make high-risk investments that you don't want to be a part of your retirement nest egg. Maybe you want to buy in to some new tech company that has potential for significant growth. The taxable brokerage account offers you numerous options outside of your foundational retirement accounts so that you can have the chance to grow your portfolio significantly, and if it fails you won't lose your nest egg for when you retire.

Another great way to expand and double down your foundation is investing in real estate. Real estate is not for everybody, but if you have the time and work ethic for it, it could become a shockingly lucrative investment.

The type of real estate I love is rental property. Rental property could be one your highest returns on investment due to the steady rental income. There are times where you may have trouble finding a tenant, but if you are strategic in the location you pick and the price you pay, you could have a cash-flowing investment for years.

As all of you have probably heard and read about real estate, there are three rules: location, location, and yes, you guessed it, location. I can 100 percent agree with this, but sometimes it's easier said than done. Often, when you find the "perfect" location, prices can be so high that the cash flow isn't there and you have to depend on the appreciation for your ROI.

Sometimes, a location looks awesome, but what about the property taxes, local politics, job outlook, natural disaster risk, and overall growth of the economy in that area? More thought should be considered than curb appeal when reviewing potential real estate deals, so be very prudent and patient.

If done correctly, real estate could definitely be a solid entry point into early retirement or further securing your retirement nest egg. What if you found a piece of property that had six units, each bringing in $1,000 a month in rent and in a very economically sound location? You could potentially bring in $4,000 net monthly income after taxes, insurance, and the mortgage have been paid. That's more than the starting salary for most entry-level jobs!

Furthermore, other types of real estate investments such house flipping, house hacking, and investing in real estate funds are great strategies to enter real estate. House flipping is quite similar to flipping cars because you buy low, fix them up to code or give them nice facelift, sell for a profit, and repeat. This could be a highly profitable business because of the huge returns you can receive if you find the right deal and manage to fix it yourself or for a very low cost and sell it based on the new appreciated value.

I am a huge fan of house hacking because whether you own your home or are looking to buy your first home, you can choose this option to subsidize or eliminate your housing expenses. The most common way this strategy works is you buy a duplex as your home, and while you live on one side of the unit, you rent out the other side for a price that equivalent to the mortgage or higher, or that is in market demand.

Maybe you didn't buy a duplex, and as you read this book, you live in a single-family home with four bedrooms and a basement. You can rent out the basement portion of your home for a decent price and subsidize your housing costs that way. Some people who are single choose to rent out every bedroom in their home and eliminate their housing costs. Overall, house hacking could become an extra stream of income to further propel your finances and secure your foundation. You can also implement house hacking when you are in the get-out-of-debt step to pay down other debts faster. Don't buy a house in that step, but if you happen to already have a home when you start this journey, it's OK to use the house hacking formula to lower your costs. You can even look into your apartment lease contract to see if they will allow you to rent out rooms in your apartment.

Regarding other real estate investments, a very easy way to enter real estate for those looking for a more hands-off approach involves buying in to different real estate funds that go out and invest in larger real estate projects. This is great for people who don't want to hassle with maintenance and worry about all of the hands-on work that goes into real estate. The most common are Real Estate Investment Trusts (REITs), and crowd funding projects.

Outside of real estate and the stock market, you can invest in other people's businesses that are privately owned. Maybe a person has a brilliant idea but lacks the necessary funds to jump-start their plans. You can lend them the required capital in exchange for a monthly payment with interest. Maybe someone has the funds, and you have the idea and you both come together to start a partnership. Partnerships have been known for ending horribly, so tread lightly when entering into business with friends or family members. I don't necessarily recommend partnerships, but these are just ideas I'm throwing around to get you thinking in the direction of other investments.

Franchises have been a very lucrative investment for people that took advantage of opening companies such as Starbucks, McDonald's, Wendy's, Burger King, etc. These are just popular ones that people see daily, but maybe you see a potential franchise that is about to take off and could be very profitable for you. Generally, we just want to think of strategic ways to be an owner of something and increase your streams of income.

The CEO of The Black Business School, Dr. Boyce Watkins once said, "One thing that's true is that whether you are making a financial investment or an investment of the heart, you usually get what you give. What's also true is that investing the wrong assets in the wrong places is a great way to end up broke (or broken)." Meaning, while investing in your passion and following your emotions may make you happy, not doing thorough research and investing strategically could end up being a terrible mistake. If the world paid you based on passion and doing what you love, most artists would be millionaires. If the world rewarded those who worked the hardest, construction workers would be the billionaires. Nothing is wrong with either career, and both are excellent fields. However, the world for the most part is a market seeking to match services and products with demand.

Final Thoughts on this Chapter
It is to be noted that everything within this step is completely up to you, and there is not a one correct way to deploy these investment vehicles. You can buy a home or rent, you can build a business or invest in a piece of a business, you can buy more real estate or rent out what you already possess. You can interchangeably and simultaneously use these strategies in a way that best fits your plans and future. Your strategy could be completely different from what was listed in this chapter. The entire

purpose of this was to promote critical thinking and determine creative ways to double down your finances and secure your financial foundation.

After you have completed this step, you can officially say that you are financially free and independent. From day one, where you started to dream and come up with a plan, to now, where your dreams are suddenly coming to fruition, you have fought and climbed from the depths of debt to creating passive income streams that allow you to be the lender and make your hard-earned money work for you.

Congratulations, and I welcome you to the next part of your life of financial independence and pursuing financial longevity. Now, the only thing left for you to do is cherish those dreams, adjust any changes needed for your future moving forward, and sustain your financially free status!

Chapter 9: Financial Freedom and Longevity

As one of the greatest investors, Warren Buffet, once said, "Someone's sitting in the shade today because someone planted a tree a long time ago." Often, we find ourselves following the crowd or latest trends whether it's socially, politically, and even financially. But I cannot stress enough one of the key factors of success and standing out from the crowd is *delayed gratification*. Finishing this financial journey the way you have is an example of a delaying one's self to later enjoy, pass on to the next generation, and create a legacy.

In the previous chapter we discussed ways to build your legacy, plant seeds, and batten down the hatches to secure your financial foundation. The importance of doubling down on your investments is sort of like insurance in case of unknown events. Now that you have secured it, the last and most critical component is sustaining what you have amassed through this entire process.

The fact that you have made it this far is further proof that you have what it takes to be financially independent. Personally, once I paid off all of my debt, I was fearful of taking on large sums of debt again. I didn't even want to take out a student loan to pay for additional college courses that I wanted to pursue. It's like after you have struggled and fought your way out of financially dependency, you never want to go back, let alone risk losing the progress you have made by borrowing more money in a cycle that landed you there in the first place.

Furthermore, the positive financial habits that you formed going through this long process often stick with you regardless. I continuously find myself using coupons, traveling on cheap airline deals, and walking to places that I need go, though I can easily spend the cash to get there. You won't look at cars, homes, and expensive dinners the same way anymore, either. You may very well be able to pay cash or take out a low-interest loan on a car, but you recognize the financial loss that cars cause after you drive them off the lot. That six-bedroom house the Joneses live in is no longer the goal, but finding a home or place to stay that fits your personal situation becomes the mission. You learn the most important thing in life is to make true decisions based on your happiness. You learn that life is about the great friends, family, and experiences you go through.

Pass it Forward

There isn't much else I can recommend at this point because everything you have experienced throughout this process has taught and led you to this position in life. I only recommend passing it forward by providing others with your wisdom, or maybe you can provide charitable donations to your church, favorite charity, or just a random person that needs a hand. Whatever it may be, remember that you were once a student, or maybe at some point you were lost. Passing it forward doesn't have to be all financial but could be just a conversation with someone in need of it. Sometimes, we get caught up in our problems but forget that others could be going through something ten times worse. That's why I wrote this book—because I want to pass forward everything I know to that person who may be falling behind in debt or wants to provide a stable future for their children or maybe just wants to live comfortable enough to escape the rat race of life.

Once you reach this stage in life, there are only a handful of things to do, and the rest is in your control. The first would be to continuously invest. Even though you have retirement accounts set up, it's OK to look into other investments as well, as we discussed in the previous chapter. Maybe you are reading this book during a very different economic time period, and there are factors you identify that may affect your situation differently. Maybe the retirement account benefits aren't as lucrative as they were during the year this book was published.

No matter the situation, just stay aware of the economic environment you are currently in, while not panicking at every sound off of bad news. Be consistent, diligent, aware, and strategic in the way you move forward to continuously invest. Whether it's stocks, bonds, crypto currencies, foreign currencies, real estate, etc., keep a level head and do the research before jumping in to anything that you do not 100 percent understand.

Update Your Will

Next, after you have exhausted all investment options, you will want to revisit your living will and estate plan that we established in the first step. Many life changes could have happened before reaching this point your life, so it's important to make any modifications that are needed to satisfy your last request when the day comes you leave this earthly life.

I always tell people: Two things are for sure after death, and that is:

1. There aren't any second chances, or rewinding back to the past. What you have done on earth is final.

2. And there is an afterlife; that is the life you leave behind, whether it's children, a spouse, friends, and other family members. This doesn't apply to everyone because some people choose to not leave anything for anyone behind. Which is perfectly fine, but I personally love the thought of remaining alive through memory and legacy even though I am no longer present on earth.

Some people choose to donate their entire estate to a charity or organization they believe in, which is also great. If you are a firm believer in discovering the cure for some form of cancer or rare disease, maybe you can donate to that cause to keep your efforts alive.

I personally would like to do a mix of things, which is totally executable. But due to my age at this time, and dependents, I must prioritize a little differently from someone who is in their seventies, for example. Taking care of my loved ones, especially if I were to leave sooner than expected, is my primary goal. Therefore, I am leaving 100 percent of my estate to my dependents and soon-to-be spouse. By the way, a dependent can be anyone that relies on you for financial support or requires your contribution to make ends meet. This is important at my age because if something were to happen to me abruptly, my family would need all the financial support they can get to keep things staying afloat.

As you modify your estate, just remember to be conscious of all the factors and variables that surround your life. And be sure to always make any changes or updates when life events happen that affect the way your estate will be executed. Don't try to go at this task alone, so please visit an attorney and accountant to work out the more detailed logistics of how your plan should be drafted. And most importantly, keep your family informed on how everything is supposed to be delegated so there aren't any fights and arguments over who was supposed to get what. Too many families have been broken for generations over something that should have been as simple as keeping everyone informed. You don't have to tell everyone the exact dollar amount or anything specific that may affect their behavior negatively, but just enough so there isn't any confusion. For example, I won't tell my eighteen-year-old son that he has $5 million waiting for him when I kick the bucket. That's a disaster waiting to happen and a spoiled brat in the making (I don't possess $5 million, this is just an example).

Review Your Life Insurance Policy

Moving forward, and more so as part two to modifying your estate, you will want to decide upon whether to terminate your life insurance policy or keep it in place. I have decided that I will continue to keep my life insurance in place due to the low-cost premium and the extra cushion it provides for my estate. I have indicated in my will that the lump sum payment from the life insurance policy must be invested and that the beneficiary will receive a monthly payout until a certain age, at which point that person will be able to do whatever they want with the entire balance. I also have other stipulations such as completion of certain financial courses and an evaluation of their personal finances, all to be handled by the executor of my estate. All of this will change when I'm married, and my spouse will be the one who ultimately controls my assets.

Now, this is completely optional, and you don't have to be as specific as me when it comes to your stipulations. You can very well terminate your life insurance policy and only pass on your home if those are your wishes. But just a reminder that at this point you have the option to discontinue the policy.

I see life insurance as a wealth-transfer instrument and an opportunity to secure your family's financial foundation further in case other assets don't work out as planned. The home you leave behind may not be able to sell as fast as you thought, or your beneficiary may decide to live in it. This will may result in them needing a source of income to sustain. Maybe your 401(k) or pension you leave behind doesn't bring in enough income for your spouse who needs to pay expensive senior living facility costs. You just never know.

Evaluate the risk, and if you feel like you need to keep it in place, great. If not, it's no big deal to terminate. If your premium is considerably cheap, I don't see any harm in keeping it around. At the end of the day it's insurance, there for you in case the uncertain or unexpected happens.

Additionally, as you work your way down the list of final tasks to do as you achieve financial longevity, you may realize that you have the extra money to donate and give more to charity, religious organizations, schools, etc. I cannot stress enough the importance of giving when you achieve some sort of financial success in life. It may have taken a lot of hard work to reach this point, but as we know with all parts of life, things can change in a matter of seconds. I'm not saying it's mandatory to pay a 10 percent tithe or give away large chunks of money to nonprofit organizations, but it may not be a bad idea to practice some form of giving. You will feel happier and have a sense of purpose, but most importantly, you will be helping people who are in need.

Sometimes when reaching such a precipitous financial point in life, many people lose purpose and meaning. You read stories of millionaires becoming drug addicts, battling depression and losing everything because at some point they lost their way. Research has even determined that money does lead to happiness, but after a certain amount it doesn't contribute to your happiness any more. In a 2010 Princeton study by Daniel Kahneman and Angus Deaton, they discovered that in the United States, making more than $75,000 per year won't significantly improve your happiness. This can vary state by state due to cost of living, but that's the average. All of this means that not only should you practice good financial habits and strategies, but also having purpose, positive relationships, and good health can greatly increase your happiness, life span, and preservation of wealth. More money is just an amplifier of who you currently are at heart. Angry people are just angrier people with money. Happy people are even happier people with money.

I'm a huge believer in passing it forward, as I stated in previous chapters, and I always try to remain humble by not giving grudgingly because at the end of the day money is a powerful tool. It can be used for the greater good or evil.

You may have noticed that I hardly mentioned "giving/tithing" throughout the process while getting out of debt. I don't advise clients on what to give or how much because I believe giving is about what your heart and spirit tell you to do. No one should command you to give something in order to find peace, be looked at as a good person, or go to "heaven." Growing up, I always heard pastors say to give a mandatory 10 percent tithe to the church, but on average the congregation was doing poorly financially or living paycheck to paycheck. This is not to say that there aren't any successful churches that have a tithing congregation that reciprocates, but from my experience, it saddened me to see members pay their tithe before paying their debt or funding their child's college fund.

If I were to recommend anything or provide any personal wisdom, I will say this: Give what you can and what you can afford. If you are struggling deeply with finances, it's perfectly fine to pause your giving to get yourself back on your feet. Sometimes it's selfish to not be selfish. A little context: in order to be able to help others, you must first help yourself so that you are in a better position to help and guide someone else. How can I advise clients on the process of getting out of debt if I never got out of debt personally? How can I advise clients on investing for their children if I don't invest for my child?

Giving may be a huge priority in your life and you may feel terrible for not giving, but think of it this way. You are temporarily pausing your giving now, to later on give at greater extents. I'm here to tell you, you will be just fine. I temporarily gave only what I could afford, and now I can give back more than ever before.

Adjust Your Lifestyle
The last step in this process is to constantly adjust your lifestyle, maintain the trajectory of building wealth, and preserve your wealth/accomplishments.

Moreover, this last step is a conclusion all of the previous steps. You will ultimately be practicing financial longevity. Even though the entire book compiles a guide to financial longevity, everything from paying off debt to being able to give back are all best practices.

The reason I titled this book *Financial Longevity* is because we often think of success as hitting the lottery, signing a contract with professional sports team, or receiving a large inheritance. However, most experts such as Dave Ramsey would argue that a great percentage of millionaires are first generation and earned most, if not all, of their wealth on their own. Financial longevity is a lifestyle, not a quick-hitting accomplishment.

I once heard the motivational entrepreneur Gary Vaynerchuk say, "I am successful not because of the end result or what I have accomplished, but because I fell in love with the process of becoming successful." What he is saying is love the process, the lifestyle, the everyday hard work ethic toward your goal.

To give context behind why I recommend continuing to adjust your lifestyle, I don't want you to become complacent and comfortable in your financial position. We live in an ever-changing world, and that commands you to be able to adapt every day. In the late 1990s, people got a little carried away during the dot-com bubble by making speculative investments and lost over 50 percent of their investments.

During the 2008 housing bubble, people started buying homes that they couldn't afford or highly speculated the amount of value they thought the house would appreciate, consequently losing tremendous amounts of money and/or even their homes. I recommend living within your means, don't make speculative investments, and adjust yourself according to the times you are currently in or approaching.

For example, when computer skills started to become a necessity, some people adapted by learning how to type and navigate the web, and others took the conspiracy approach that the computers were evil. Those people that didn't adapt couldn't land a job as easily as someone who was adaptable.

Maintaining and preserving your wealth work hand-in-hand and should continue as an everyday practice no matter your financial status. It can become comforting to see $100,000 in your investment portfolio, and you may say you don't want to be part of the super-rich or that you're not greedy, but the reality is you will need well over that amount to retire. So, don't go and buy a $90,000 Mercedes-Benz in cash just because you have the cash to do so. Remain conscious of how hard you worked to achieve some sort of financial freedom, and do your very best to preserve that status.

Eventually, the day will come when you will retire, if you haven't already done so, and your hard work and investments will take care you and your family. Don't allow quick impulses to destroy everything you have worked for.

It's always interesting to see how financial freedom and success stories are fun to read. However, the hardest part for most people is simply starting. Even I struggled to start, but when I encountered trauma in my life and hit rock bottom, I woke up and got to work.

I want you to be inspired, energized, and excited to pursue the goals within this book. I want you to change the cycle in your family and create a new path for generations after you. We are all here to do many things, and I am firm believer that one of those many things is to pass on the torch to the next living generation. Whether it is your children, a mentee, a younger sibling, or a complete stranger that just needs a helping hand, be there for them to pass it forward.

Finance is a significant part of life, which is why I teach it and help people with it. When was the last time you didn't need money to pay the rent or mortgage? When was the last time you didn't need money to buy food, clothing, or mandatory goods? If you answered never, please call me so that I can do whatever it is you are doing.

However, for those of us who need money on daily basis to survive, take note of the points this book outlines. Realize the importance of money, and make it a priority to adopt this lifestyle of financial longevity. Money isn't everything but rather a means to an end and a tool that gets you from point A to point B.

It is my hope that after digesting this book that you were able to add value to your life and chart a clear direction to become confident with money. Making it to the end of this book is proof that you are capable of achieving financial freedom because why else would you read it? Once you finish this book, maybe you can pass it on or refer others to read it that may be struggling with personal finance. It is also my hope that younger people can read this book as soon as possible so that they can fast-forward through the debt-free step and get started on building their emergency fund.

Wherever you may find yourself in life, be it overwhelmed in debt, struggling with credit issues, or worried about retirement, I'm here to help, and so are a plethora of other financial coaches who are willing to assist you. Just steer clear of the ones who may make it sound a little too easy.

Thank you for reading, and good luck on your quest to financial longevity!

Brief Recap and Checklist of All Financial Longevity Steps

✓ Start by creating a written plan, budget, and long-term goals.

✓ Check credit report from all three bureaus (Equifax, Transunion, and Experian).

✓ Start a life insurance policy, enroll in a health insurance/short-term disability plan (if needed), create an estate plan.

✓ Continue to invest in your employer retirement plan up to the employer match, then stop contributing once you have reached that point. If your income is low and can only handle basic necessities, temporarily pause all retirement contributions until you have money to set aside.

✓ Create a Rainy Day Fund by opening a high-yield savings account and depositing up to one month's worth of expenses.

✓ Eliminate all debt, collections, and other financial obligations except the mortgage.

✓ Turn your Rainy Day Fund into a Stormy Day Fund by depositing an extra two to twelve months' worth of expenses into it. You can have more than twelve months if that's your preference.

✓ Draft a retirement plan to determine when, where, and how you wish to retire.

✓ Implement your retirement plan by investing 15 percent or more of your income in retirement accounts such as 401(k), IRA, HSA, etc. If your income is above average, attempt to max out most of your retirement accounts up to the federal limits. If your income is below average, start small by contributing 5 percent and increase by a percentage point every month or every other month.

✓ Pay off your mortgage early, if applicable.

✓ Buy a home or continue to rent. Postponing home ownership until you have the cash to purchase a home in full isn't a bad option.

✓ Fund children's college or investment accounts, if applicable.

✓ Create an Asset Snowball. This can be a new or existing business, taxable brokerage account, and/or other creative passive income streams.

✓ Increase your charitable giving, donations, and/or volunteer work.

✓ Continuously learn and work on personal development.

✓ Modify your estate plan.

✓ Continue to invest for retirement.

✓ Preserve and sustain your wealth.

✓ Live a life of financial longevity.

About the Author

Danterious Owens, better known as Dan, operates a web-based business called DanTheMentor.com. There, he assists clients from all walks of life with achieving their personal financial goals, and most importantly, their life's ambitions. He believes that personal finance ties in with all parts of life and hopes that people can one day view money as a means to an end rather than the main objective.

Dan lives in the Lone Star State with his soon-to-be spouse Glorieuse, and their son Danterious Jr. He was born and raised in the small town of Clarksdale, Mississippi, known to many as the "Home of the Blues." After spending his early childhood mainly in Mississippi, his mother, Erica, relocated with him and his brother Erion to Normal, IL, where Dan would later start his insurance career.

Dan attended high school at Normal Community High School and Clarksdale High School. Later, he went to complete his college education at Northwest Mississippi Community College, Coahoma Community College, and Mississippi Valley State University.

My Notes and Ideas

Use these pages to record your thoughts and ideas while reading this book:

NOTES

NOTES

www.ingramcontent.com/pod-product-compliance
Lightning Source LLC
Chambersburg PA
CBHW071304220526
45468CB00001B/269